WHAT ARE THEY SAYING
ABOUT THE RESURRECTION?

What Are They Saying about the Resurrection?

by
Gerald O'Collins, S.J.

PAULIST PRESS
New York/Ramsey/Toronto

ACKNOWLEDGMENTS

In a slightly different form the third chapter of this book appeared in *The Way*, a quarterly review of contemporary Christian spirituality, published by the English Jesuits, under the title: *Jesus in Current Theology* III appearing in the issue of April 1977 (Vol. 17, No. 2). The Appendix of this book—also in a slightly different form—was published in *Heythrop Journal* for 1971 (Vol. 12, No. 3). Both pieces are reprinted by permission.

Unless otherwise indicated, the scriptural texts in this book are taken from the Revised Standard Version of the Bible, copyrighted 1946 and 1952 by the Division of Christian Education of the National Council of Churches and used by permission.

The abbreviation ET, used primarily in the Notes, means English Translation.

Library of Congress
Catalog Card Number: 78-51594

ISBN: 0-8091-2109-3

Published by Paulist Press
Editorial Office: 1865 Broadway, New York, N.Y. 10023
Business Office: 545 Island Road, Ramsey, N.J. 07446

Printed and bound in the
United States of America

Contents

Preface

On any reckoning the resurrection of Jesus
Christ is one of the key doctrines of Christianity.
The Apostles' Creed, the Nicene Creed and other
classic professions of faith all include the resurrection among the principal points of belief. Such
creeds are recited at baptism, in the celebration of
the Eucharist, at the vigil service on Holy Saturday
and on other occasions. Many prayers, hymns,
sermons, catechisms and paintings join together in
proclaiming the same joyful message: "Dying you
destroyed our death; rising you restored our life.
Lord Jesus, come in glory." Christians live their
lives "in memory of his death and resurrection."

Each year millions of people see on television
or hear on the radio the Pope's Easter broadcast
from Rome. In a variety of languages the Pope announces, "Christ is risen, Alleluia!" At Easter
1977, Pope Paul VI dwelt on the theme of newness.
"A new world is founded; a new way of existing is
inaugurated. Christ is risen; Christ lives!" The resurrection of the Lord shows that bodily death is
only "the dream which precedes a new day that has
no sunset."

For me the Pope's words recalled the Holy
Saturday liturgy. In the vigil service a new paschal

candle stands in the sanctuary. There are fresh cloths and flowers on the altar. The celebrant blesses new baptismal water. During the Mass he consecrates new hosts. In these and other ways the liturgy expresses the cause of our Easter joy: "The Lord is risen from the dead, and all things are made new."

We may take newness or something else (like freedom from fear) as the major key in which we interpret the Lord's resurrection. In any case we should have little difficulty about agreeing that the Lord's resurrection is central for Christian faith. The life, liturgy, creeds, and day-to-day faith of Christians testify to that.

It may, however, come as a surprise to some readers that no general council of the Church or Pope has ever solemnly proclaimed some particular doctrine on Christ's resurrection. A council has never met to form and fashion some teaching in response to a heresy concerning the Lord's rising from the dead. A living consensus, expressed by the common creeds, has sufficed for two thousand years. In their turn these creeds clearly echo the New Testament and, specifically, the kind of concise confession of faith which we find in 1 Corinthians 15:3f.: "I delivered to you as of first importance what I also received, that Christ died for our sins in accordance with the Scriptures, that he was buried, that he was raised on the third day in accordance with the Scriptures." In effect, for our interpretation of what Christ's resurrection means we have no solemn "magisterial" statements to guide us, but largely depend on two other sources: (a) the ordinary life and teaching of the Church, and (b) the New Testament texts.

We know *that* we and millions of others believe (and have believed) in Christ as risen from the dead. But we may not be quite so clear *what* it is that we believe when we profess our faith at this point. We could feel a little like St. Augustine when he took up the topic of time in his *Confessions*: "What, then, is time? I know well enough what it is, provided that nobody asks me. But if I am asked what it is and try to explain, I am baffled" (Bk. XI, ch. 14). We can think we know well enough what Christ's "rising from the dead" is, but we may become baffled if pressed for an explanation.

Worse than that, news may filter back about debates and disagreements among theologians. It can be unnerving and depressing to find that the experts fail to agree about the Lord's resurrection. What St. Paul happily announced as good news (1 Cor. 15:1) turns out then to be a cause of worry and the occasion of scandalous confusion.

However, not all apparently conflicting interpretations of the resurrection really collide. Here I do not wish to cheat and pretend that there are neither genuine debates nor truly irreconcilable positions. Nevertheless, there are fewer real differences than might appear at first glance.

What we meet in the Lord's resurrection is a multidimensional mystery. No one account can ever hope to be exhaustive. It would be a false procedure to isolate one formulation and take that to be *the* exclusive explanation. To a large extent, what we find in the writing on the resurrection by Karl Barth, Raymond Brown, Rudolf Bultmann, Xavier Léon-Dufour, Jürgen Moltmann, Wolfhart Pannenberg and others are different points of orientation toward the same mystery of the resurrection. Their interests and views often prove complementary rather than contradictory.

Somewhere John Henry Newman remarks: "As we cannot see the whole starry firmament at once, but have to turn ourselves from east to west, sighting first one constellation and then another, and losing these in order to gain those, so it is, and much more, with such real apprehension as we can secure of the divine nature." Many Roman Catholics and other Christians have long ago made their peace with this approach when they reflect on such mysteries as the Trinity, the Eucharist and the Church. One generation sights the truth that the Church is the body of Christ, while another generation sights the truth that the Church forms the people of God. Sixteenth-century Catholics saw the Eucharist as sacrifice. Twentieth-century Catholics see the Eucharist as meal. St. Augustine interpreted the Trinity according to a psychological model of human knowing and loving. The Son is generated as the Father's act of thinking, and the Holy Spirit "proceeds" as the mutual love of the Father and the Son. A contemporary theologian, Heribert Mühlen, applies interpersonal categories to the Trinity and speaks of the Father, Son and Holy Spirit as respectively the I-, Thou- and We- relations within the divine nature.

My point here is this. We have become used to the idea that—as regards the divine nature, the Church, the Eucharist and the Trinity—some given interpretation may contain a good deal of truth but will never exhaust the truth. It is high time to apply this insight to Christ's resurrection. Hence the first chapter of this little book is entitled "Models of the Resurrection."

If this work begins by indicating how points of interest can converge, the second chapter identifies and discusses several current questions. On the one hand, is the New Testament language about Christ's resurrection really only a way of referring to the rise of faith? Or on the other hand, should we insist on the *literal* truth of all the details in the Gospel stories of Easter? Do later Christians experience the risen Christ in the same way as did Peter, Paul and the other "official" Easter witnesses? Should we take any of the words attributed to the risen Lord as authentic or literally deriving from him? Does "resurrection" differ from or merge with "exaltation"? And, for that matter, what are the right terms to use of Christ's resurrection (physical, historical and bodily, or spiritual, transhistorical and symbolic)?

The third and fourth chapters draw attention to some areas and approaches which promise to enrich any theology of the resurrection: for instance, the right use of the imagination and the significance of Peter as the first Easter witness. These seem to be among valuable growth points for theological reflection about the Lord's resurrection.

In an appendix, I include a revised version of my review of Willi Marxsen's *The Resurrection of Jesus of Nazareth* (Philadelphia, 1970). Leo Scheffczyk's *Auferstehung: Prinzip Christlichen Glaubens* (Einsiedeln, 1976) and other recent studies suggest that—since the late 1960's—Marxsen has replaced Bultmann as the archprotagonist in debates about the resurrection.

Finally, I want to thank warmly Raymond Brown, John Keating, Edward Malatesta, John Reilly, Catharine Stewart Roache and Dennis Sheehan, as well as other friends, colleagues and students in Italy, the United States and elsewhere. Their questions and comments have prodded me into clarifying some obscurities and attaining some higher viewpoints. I am grateful to Sister M. Charlene Schneider, S.S.N.D., for her generosity and skill in typing most of the original manuscript. This book is affectionately dedicated to John and Judith O'Neill in admiration and gratitude.

The Gregorian University
Rome
October 20, 1977

1
Models of the Resurrection

At times theologians can show themselves willing to exploit minor difficulties and differences in order to win a place in the scholarly sun. There is normally no prize for reporting either a genuine consensus or the converging lines of general orientations.

In editing his *Diskussion um Kreuz und Auferstehung* (Wuppertal, 1967), however, Bertold Klappert has rendered "lasting service to the academic and pastoral evaluation of the issues" concerning Christ's death and resurrection. Through his own introductory essay and a series of excerpted articles from Barth, Bultmann, Moltmann and others, Klappert shows how the Lord's resurrection both admits a *pluriformity* of converging interpretative models and "transcends them all in its concrete reality."[1] He is neither deceiving himself nor using his scholarship as a way of advancing his own apologetic purposes. We should acknowledge here the existence and value of multiple *models*: the resurrection (1) as history, (2) as redemption, (3) as revelation, (4) as grounding faith, (5) as a promise which grounds hope, and (6) as initiating the kerygma.

Klappert himself does not list revelation as a separate heading. Furthermore, he speaks of the "aspects" of the resurrection event. He notes the "multidimensionality" of the resurrection reports in the New Testament. Some might decide to adopt his terminology and talk of different aspects or dimensions of a mystery which can never be fully and finally expressed. However, I prefer to speak here of models of the resurrection.

In his *Models of the Church* (New York, 1974) Avery Dulles has persuasively indicated the advantages of model-terminology over aspect-terminology. Moreover, those readers who know in detail the work of the theologians to be cited in this chapter will appreciate that mostly they offer multi-dimensional and complex, if coherent, versions of the resurrection. Hence to speak of them as attending to just one aspect of the mystery of Christ's resurrection would fail to do justice to the rich, in-depth quality of their work.

Whether we decide to opt for "aspects" or "models," Klappert has, in any case, alerted us to a highly important feature of twentieth-century work on Christ's resurrection. Despite all their debates and polemic, many scholars have not in fact been simply on collision course with each other. They have specialized in one or other model in reflecting on that many-faceted mystery which is the Lord's rising from the dead. This chapter aims to build on

Klappert's insights and to discuss contemporary orientations under the six headings indicated above.

I
SIX INTERPRETATIVE MODELS

The Resurrection as History

The heading of "history" gathers together the contributions of many exegetes and theologians. Here belong names like Raymond Brown, C. F. Evans, Reginald Fuller, Xavier Léon-Dufour, Wolf- ✓ hart Pannenberg, Norman Perrin, and Béda Rigaux. They take up 1 Corinthians 15, the closing chapters of the Gospels, and other New Testament texts dealing with the Lord's resurrection to investigate what can be known about them historically. How did these texts get into their final shape? What sources did Paul and the evangelists have at their disposal? What editorial arrangements and theological reflections do they appear to have added *either* to the oral and written material that came to them *or* to the basic data of their own personal experience? Brown and other such scholars wish to push back from the New Testament texts (written in the mid- or late-first century) through the early decades in the life of the Christian communities to settle what can be settled about the things which happened soon after the crucifixion of Jesus. The key question is this: How far can a balanced historical inquiry take us in deciding not only how the basic documents about Christ's resurrection were formed but also what events lie behind these texts?

This first paragraph on "the resurrection as history" has spoken of "events," "historical inquiry" and, of course, "history." Some readers will want me to delineate more sharply and clearly what I mean by "history" and how I understand its limits. Let me refer them to Chapter Five of my *The Resurrection of Jesus Christ* (Valley Forge, 1973) and the several relevant chapters in my *Foundations of Theology* (Chicago, 1971). Here let me simply state that those who investigate history have the task of tracing the causes and results of meaningful events that in one way or another happen in and/or to our world of space and time. This version of history may sound rather wide and fluid. However, I am *not* attempting here to work out precisely my own understanding of "history" and then apply it to the resurrection, in order to show how "history" so conceived might or might not function as a model of the resurrection. I must leave matters somewhat broad because I am dealing with a range of scholars who are by no means unanimous in their judgments on the nature of history. At most their views on history show a certain family resemblance.

What conclusions have those theologians reached who take an historical perspective and develop this model of the resurrection as history? In a review of my *The Resurrection of Jesus Christ* Fuller has drawn attention to a consensus which has emerged among a number of recent writers on the resurrection (Brown, Fuller himself, Léon-Dufour, Pannenberg, myself and others). With various nuances adopted by individual authors, the consensus includes at least the following items:

> It is generally agreed that the starting point for any investigation of the Easter traditions lies not in the narratives at the ends of the Gospels, but in 1 Corinthians 15. This establishes the earliest tradition of the appearances. These appearances are to be interpreted not as encounters with a resuscitated Jesus prior to an ascension, but as eschatological disclosures "from heaven" of an already exalted One. The empty tomb was not part of the kerygma cited by Paul, nor does Easter faith rest upon it, yet the empty tomb pericopes rest upon an ancient historical nucleus. Mary Magdalene, at least, found an empty grave. The resurrection itself, never witnessed or narrated, was an eschatological event between God and Jesus ("God raised Jesus from the dead"), not merely something that happened to the disciples. Jesus was translated at his resurrection into an entirely new mode of existence, to be sharply distinguished from the kind of resuscitations alleged of Jairus' daughter, the widow of Naim's son, or Lazarus.[2]

Those who study the resurrection as history do more than provide a set of particular conclusions which form a modest but important consensus.

They also forcefully remind us that we should never emancipate faith from its historical origins. A belief in the risen Christ that in principle excluded all historical inquiry about the events immediately following the crucifixion would suppress an essential dimension of the Christian faith. This faith commits itself in the light of certain realities which took place prior to our commitment and independently of it (*ante nos* and *extra nos*). We may not jump the gun of historical criticism. In its healthy forms such criticism represents a legitimate development in the historical world-view that belongs to the Jewish-Christian faith from its beginnings.

Hence it prompts misgivings when some scholars who deal with the resurrection as history pull back from pursuing their inquiries to the end. They identify and study the contributions of the New Testament authors. They seek to reconstruct the preaching about the crucified and risen Lord in the early years of the Church. But then a few writers like C. F. Evans refuse to commit themselves about the *cause* of that preaching and the traditions on which Paul and the Gospel writers were to draw. Evans states: "Whatever the Easter event was, it must be supposed to be of such a kind as to be responsible for the production of these traditions as its deposit at whatever remove."[3] The repeated "whatever" leaves the Easter event thoroughly unspecified—both in its nature and in its proximity to the results ("at whatever remove"). The position adopted comes to this: The cause (whether remote or proximate) must have been sufficient to produce the historical effects (the early Christian traditions). Such a cautious statement can hardly be denied. But is it sufficient? It tells us nothing specific about the external world of history and nature, and merely recalls the fact that our understanding spontaneously interprets in that way the data which it receives. Every effect must have a cause. Evans leaves the Easter event as a kind of Kantian noumenon, veiled forever behind the visible, historical data. While not sharing our modern historical preoccupations, the New Testament does, however, point to the major cause which produced the Easter traditions. Primarily it took the form of the appearance (to Peter, Paul and others) of the risen Lord. There seems to be no effective reason why those whose interests are essentially historical should flinch from fully tracing the genesis of the Easter message and nominating the cause or causes behind that message. It seems odd to play the historian and then stop short in one's examination of the causality.

Those who take Evans' line would presumably argue that any attempt to get behind the early Christian traditions and investigate alleged appearances of the risen Lord would move us beyond the controllable, empirical evidence. Hence these traditions constitute the natural frontier for *historical* inquiry. I wonder. The appearances are presented as something that happened to a number of people (Peter, Paul, Mary Magdalene and others, both individuals and groups). The places (for instance, Galilee and the Damascus road) and the times (for instance, the Easter day itself) are sometimes specified in our sources. These alleged appearances have controllable, empirical results in the lives of the witnesses. In principle, therefore, I find no convincing argument against examining historically the supposed encounters between the disciples and the risen Christ. In practice, the evidence remains limited, as I point out in Chapter Six of *The Resurrection of Jesus Christ*. Nevertheless, it is a legitimate *historical* task to investigate the Easter events in the sense of asking what happened to the disciples.

Before we leave the model of resurrection as history, two further matters call for attention. Robert C. Ware points out how new perspectives on the nature of history have modified the study of the resurrection as history. The emphasis has shifted from "a positivistic-minded historical approach" (which doggedly concentrates simply on the concrete data and their causes) to "a more phenomenological perspective concerned with understanding 'facts' and their meaning." Shifts in ways of interpreting the study of history in general should affect the work of those who deal with the resurrection as history. The appendix to this book takes up this point apropos of Marxsen's version of the resurrection.

Ware's observation on recent changes in the understanding of history calls for one important qualification. We may adopt a "more phenomenological perspective" and concern ourselves with "understanding 'facts' and their meaning." Nevertheless, in the case of the resurrection the "facts" must always be recognized to be of a special quality. So too will be our interpretation of them. No shift in our theoretical perspective on history is going to yield more than a certain (limited) similarity between these facts and those of everyday, or even scientific, experience.

Secondly, Ware warns us against letting our appreciation of Christ's resurrection become "lured into a one-sided historical-critical perspective."[4] We could put this point less solemnly. Historical truth is not the only kind of truth. As regards both the resurrection and other themes concerned with the concrete reality of Jesus Christ, it would normally be a disastrous error to adopt the principle that what is not historical is, therefore, unreal. To express matters positively, everything that is historical is real, but not everything that is real is historical. Nuclear or particle physicists offer an obvious example. They have postulated and discovered many carriers of mass and carriers of energy: electrons, protons, mesons, gluons and the rest, the rest including those engaging and elusive characters, the quarks. The actual discovery of an extra quark can rate as an historical (or even an historic) event. But the precise number of quarks is simply a fact, truth or reality of nature. Further examples abound to illustrate the difference between the real and the historical. God's existence, for instance, is a truth of reality but not an historical truth. Jesus' parable of the Good Samaritan truly describes reality, but it does not report some (very minor) historical episode. However we work this out in detail, we should admit a distinction between the real and the historical and allow this distinction to be operative in our analysis.

Then, of course, some may be tempted to merge the real and the historical by giving history a very broad definition and making it, as Pannenberg does, more or less co-terminous with reality. Here I do not want to engage in an enormous parenthesis and review those accounts of history which take this line. Let me simply note this. The particular way in which Pannenberg follows Hegel and develops a scheme of universal history entails neglecting the theme of *mystery*. In his classic *Jesus—God and Man* he has nothing to say either about the resurrection as mystery or, for that matter, about the mystery involved in any other doctrine concerned with Christ. His version of the resurrection within the limits of historical reason alone fails to cope with its mystery.

The Resurrection as Redemption

The successes of the scholars who have specialized in what I call "the resurrection as history" have unwittingly reinforced a widespread tendency to consider the Lord's rising from the dead within the limits of history alone. Both those who accept this resurrection and those who deny it often show themselves content to settle the facts for their own satisfaction. They give their answers to the question posed by the title of Frank Morison's book *Who Moved the Stone?* and leave it at that. Yet the historical model provides only one of the maps to guide our exploration of the resurrection. Christians and interested non-Christians alike need to be coaxed into recognizing further possible models. The Lord's resurrection presents itself as a reality not only "before us" *(ante nos)* and "beyond us" *(extra nos)* but also "for us" *pro nobis).*

Anyone who read Catholic theological and exegetical works from the 1950's will remember a stream of articles and books on the saving value of Christ's resurrection from such writers as F. X. Durrwell, Stanislas Lyonnet and David Stanley. These scholars took their inspiration at least partly from a rediscovered theme in St. Thomas Aquinas. His commentaries on Paul's letters, along with sections on the resurrection in the *Summa Theologica*, served to alert them to the essential role which Christ's resurrection plays in our justification.[5] At the Pontifical Biblical Institute, Stanley defended in 1952 his doctoral thesis which was later published under the title *Christ's Resurrection in Pauline Soteriology*. Durrwell's *The Resurrection* had its first (French) edition in 1950, and Lyonnet's important article, "La valeur sotériologique de la résurrection du Christ selon saint Paul," appeared in the *Gregorianum* for 1958. They effectively rebuked their theological predecessors and contemporaries for forgetting that Christ was not only put to death for our sins but also raised again for our justification (Rom. 4:25).

Advances in biblical studies and theology have rendered obsolete some of the positions argued or presupposed by Durrwell and others. Nevertheless, those who developed the model of resurrection as salvation or redemption contributed some enduringly valuable insights: for instance, the progressively deeper understanding of Christ's resurrection which we find in St. Paul's letters. Stanley encourages us to note the development in the apostle's reflections on the "timing," the beneficiaries and the "causality" of the resurrection. This development emerges from a comparison between passages in 1 Thessalonians, 2 Corinthians and Romans.

In 1 Thessalonians 4:13-18 Paul writes:

> But we would not have you ignorant, brethren, concerning those who are asleep, that you may not grieve as others do who have no hope. For since we believe that Jesus died and rose again, even so, through Jesus, God will bring with him those who have fallen asleep. For this we declare to you by the word of the Lord, that we who are alive, who are left until the coming of the Lord, shall not precede those who have fallen asleep. For the Lord himself will descend from heaven with a cry of command, with the archangel's call, and with the sound of the trumpet of God. And the dead in Christ will rise first; then we who are alive, who are left, shall be caught up together with them in the clouds

to meet the Lord in the air; and so we shall always be with the Lord. Therefore comfort one another with these words.

In this, his earliest letter (c. A.D. 50) Paul's appeal to the resurrection fuels a *future* perspective. The saving impact of Jesus' rising from the dead concerns what God *will* do: both for those who will be alive at "the coming of the Lord" and for those "who have fallen asleep." It is then that the living and the dead will experience the power of the resurrection, being "caught up" to be "always with the Lord." To express this "timing" in technical terms, the purpose of the Lord's resurrection is eschatological—in the sense of futurist eschatology. Paul mentions the *past* events of Good Friday and Easter Sunday ("Jesus died and rose again"), but says nothing here about the resurrection's influence upon present Christian existence. The change *will come* at the parousia. The apostle understands the beneficiaries of that transformation to be Christians (the "brethren" and "the dead in Christ"). He speaks of the death and resurrection of Jesus and expresses his belief that God's final intervention will happen "through Jesus," but he does not explain how the "causality" will operate for our salvation, present or future.

    Paul's understanding has clearly gained ground by the time he wrote 2 Corinthians (c. A.D. 55 or 56).[6] He now appreciates the resurrection's influence upon *present* life: "He died for all, that those who live might live no longer for themselves but for him who for their sake died and was raised" (2 Cor. 5:15). The beneficiaries of the Lord's death and resurrection are universalized: "He died for all." But Paul leaves unexplained what Stanley calls the "causality."

Finally in Romans—the masterly version of the good news which he wrote around A.D. 57—Paul sees the purpose of Christ's death and resurrection to be both present and future salvation. That dying and rising have resulted in a new life communicated through faith and baptism: "We were buried with him by baptism into death, so that as Christ was raised from the dead by the glory of the Father, we too might walk in newness of life" (Rom. 6:4). This salvation experience now provides the basis for future or eschatological salvation: "If we have been united with him in a death like his, we shall certainly be united with him in a resurrection like his" (Rom. 6:5). Romans 8:11 ties together present and future salvation as the outcome of the Lord's death and resurrection: "If the Spirit of him who raised Jesus from the dead dwells in you, he who raised Christ Jesus from the dead will give life to your mortal bodies also through his Spirit which dwells in you."

In Romans Paul clarifies the beneficiaries of Christ's death and resurrection. They are not only the Christians "buried with him by baptism" (Rom. 6:4f.), but also Israel and indeed the whole created world. The apostle expounds Israel's present "rejection" and future admission to God's kingdom as a kind of dying and rising (11:15). In a state of bondage to decay the creation now waits and groans for future transformation (8:19ff.). To complete the picture, Romans explicitly associates the "causality" of Christ's resurrection with that of his death in effecting salvation: "It [righteousness] will be reckoned to us who believe in him who raised from the dead Jesus our Lord, who was put to death for our trespasses and raised for our justification" (4:24f.). The crucifixion and the resurrection operate jointly as causes bringing about our total redemption.

All in all, Stanley has proposed an enduringly useful scheme for tracing the development in St. Paul's reflections on the impact of Christ's death *and resurrection*: the "timing" (present justification and eschatological salvation), the "beneficiaries" and the "causality."

So far we have recalled Catholic scholars whose interests have swung toward the resurrection as redemption. Among Protestant theologians Karl Barth stands out for his contributions on the redemptive function of Christ's resurrection. Ernest Hemingway remarks somewhere that praising one writer to another is like mentioning one general favorably to another general: "You learn not to do it the first time you make the mistake." Sad to say, something like this is true of some theologians. You learn to be careful in choosing the theologians you mention favorably to other theologians. Nowadays it is in some circles a "mistake" to praise Barth and his theology of the resurrection. It has become con-

ventional to dismiss his contribution by pointing to
his dubious claim on the historical nature of Easter.
He attributes genuine historical character to the
resurrection and yet denies historians the right to
pronounce on the matter! Nevertheless, Barth's reflections on Christ's resurrection enjoy a permanent
value—not least for his massive reminder that our
theology will be drastically impoverished if we
forget the function of the resurrection in the divine
plan for reconciliation. At great length he explains
how the "yes of the reconciling will of God" has
been both "effective and expressed" through
Christ's resurrection.[7]

In treating the resurrection as redemption some
writers have sought to illustrate what the experience of resurrection could be like now. Admittedly
this is only one aspect of the resurrection's redemptive function, but it is a vitally important dimension.
To speak of Jesus' rising from the dead will in the
long run prove unintelligible and unacceptable, unless our own lives allow us to experience now something of that resurrection and its power to transform
us. Hence in *The Resurrection of Jesus Christ* (Valley Forge, 1973) I developed what I call "the expe-
riential correlate" of the resurrection.

In his *True Resurrection* (New York, 1972)
H. A. Williams offers some wonderful examples of
how the resurrection could be experienced in life.
No one can fail to be exhilarated, informed, and
challenged by this book. At the same time, however, his insistence on present experience occasionally leads him to undervalue the past and the

future. He maintains, for instance: "Like all theory, the future has no teeth" (p. 5). I wonder. The work of Viktor Frankl on meaning and William Lynch on hope has shown how necessary for survival and growth the future is. In recent decades the world has repeatedly witnessed what dragon's teeth the future has for dedicated revolutionaries. A hope for tomorrow's victory can prove far more powerful than any joyful or disheartening experiences of to-day.

Nevertheless, Williams' book forcefully serves to remind us that we will truly believe in the resurrection only if we know the risen Christ as a living force in our lives. In John 11:21-27 Martha assures Jesus of her conviction that her dead brother will rise in the resurrection at the last day. But that is not enough for Jesus: "I *am* the resurrection and the life: he who believes in me, though he die, yet shall he live" (v. 25). Resurrection faith is fully real only when it is a faith experience of Jesus now. What Martha says is not denied, but it finds its proper basis in the recognition that Jesus lives now for her.

Alice in Wonderland expresses in a comic way the kind of point which should be made about the resurrection as redemption or—if you like—the risen Christ as saving and redeeming. Part of Alice's conversation with the White Queen goes like this:

> " . . . and I don't care for jam."
> "It's very good jam," said the Queen.
> "Well, I don't want any *to-day*, at any rate."

"You couldn't have it if you *did* want it," the Queen said. "The rule is, jam to-morrow and jam yesterday—but never jam *to-day*."

"It *must* come sometimes to 'jam to-day,' " Alice objected.

"No, it can't," said the Queen. "It's jam every *other* day: to-day isn't any other day, you know."

Many theologians have resembled the Queen in laying down "the rule" that there was resurrection yesterday (Christ's), there will be resurrection to-morrow (the general resurrection at the end), but there is never resurrection today. With skill and insight Williams has put the case precisely for resurrection today.

Let me make a final point before leaving the model of the resurrection as redemption. It would be a mistake to think of Christ's incarnation, life, death and resurrection as transient episodes mediating grace. Both now and for all eternity we find the living God through the humanity of Christ. Karl Rahner[8] has rightly insisted on the way that the risen and glorified Christ remains the mediator of salvation for all eternity. The Word who became flesh to die and rise was, is, and continues forever to be the "hinge" of our salvation. We can apply here Tertullian's classic phrase *caro cardo salutis* (the flesh is the hinge of salvation). The Lord's rising from the dead was not only historically *ante nos* and *extra nos*, but also redemptively and enduringly "for us and for our salvation."

The Resurrection as Revelation

A number of significant contributions to the theology of the resurrection cluster together under the heading of "revelation." I think here of Barth during his dialectical stage, of Bultmann, of Moltmann's *The Crucified God* (German original 1972) and of Pannenberg.

Both as regards Christ's resurrection and elsewhere in theology the notion of revelation and redemption intertwine almost inextricably. To speak of God's revealing activity is to speak of his redemptive activity and vice versa. John's Gospel strikingly exemplifies how the truth revealed in Christ and the life offered by him are but two sides of the one coin—God's living self-communication. In saving us Christ reveals himself and his Father. By his revelation Christ saves us. Pannenberg puts it this way:

> The correlation of revelation and salvation cannot be discussed in detail here, since we are primarily concerned with the fundamental structure of revelation. However, the fact of this connection is presupposed throughout. . . . For the man who is disposed to an openness toward God, revelation in its deepest sense means salvation, fulfillment of his destiny and his very being. . . . The revelation of God truly speaks to the sinner.[9]

Nevertheless, a given theologian, as in the case of Pannenberg, may focus on revelation much more

than on salvation. Hence we are justified in distin-
guishing "the resurrection as revelation" from "the
resurrection as redemption"—provided, of course,
that we admit the strong family resemblance between the two models.

To return to the names listed above. Barth's
Epistle to the Romans in its second edition of 1921
marked the real beginning of twentieth-century theology, or at least of twentieth-century Protestant
theology. Barth decisively rejected the liberal theology he had learned from Adolf von Harnack and
his other teachers, turned to paradox and dialectical
thinking, and then with his study of Anselm (*Fides
Quaerens Intellectum*, 1931) rethought his theological task in terms not only of "faith seeking understanding" but also of an uncompromising Christo-
centrism. The key to the theological revolution
Barth initiated in the 1920's was his discovery of
"the revelation of God as the decisive category of
theological thought." He called on his readers and
hearers to take revelation seriously, namely as that
ultimate "crisis" which confronts human beings
when God makes himself known. "God has spoken
(*Deus dixit*)"—over and over again Barth recalled
the revealing word of God which the believer hears
and the theologian elucidates. "It is not," he explained, "the right human thoughts about God
which form the content of the Bible, but the right
divine thoughts about men. The Bible tells us not
how we should talk about God but what he says to
us."[10]

Given the almost unqualified dominance as-
signed to the category of revelation during his

dialectical period, it occasions little surprise to find that Barth developed then the model of resurrection as revelation. In his *The Resurrection of the Dead* he declared that resurrection "as such is only to be grasped in the category of revelation and none other." It expressed the "miracle" which God performed (and performs) in revealing himself to humanity.[11] Barth made similar assertions in his *Epistle to the Romans*: "The resurrection is the revelation; the disclosing of Jesus as the Christ, the appearing of God and the apprehending of God in Jesus."[12] The resurrection was not merely credited with a central function in revelation. It was absorbed into revelation.

The later Barth declined to interpret Christ's resurrection simply and exclusively through the model of revelation. The revelatory function remained essential, but the resurrection was no longer merged into revelation. This final phase of Barth's thought was definitively inaugurated with the publication of the first volume of *Church Dogmatics* in 1932. From the early to the later volumes we meet a reiterated insistence on the historical reality of the resurrection and the appearances of the risen Christ. These appearances formed the "Archimedean point" upon which all biblical witness rested.[13] The "central," "indispensable" place which the historical event of the resurrection held in the New Testament found expression in the following terms:

While we could imagine a New Testament containing only the history of Easter and its message, we could not possibly imagine a New Testament without it. For the history and message of Easter contains everything else, while without it everything else would be left in the air as a mere abstraction. . . . It is the key to the whole. . . . Either we believe with the New Testament in the risen Jesus Christ, or we do not believe in him at all.[14]

The later Barth was no longer satisfied to use exclusively the category of revelation and speak simply of the ''message'' of the resurrection. Such an expression could have appeared to have reduced the resurrection merely to its revelatory value and its function in the Church's preaching. Barth wanted to safeguard the actual occurrence of the resurrection as history. The model of the resurrection as revelation or ''message'' no longer proved sufficient for him.

I have dwelt on Barth because he represents a lively example of a theologian who turned away from an exclusive use of one model of the resurrection. Let me now comment on Bultmann, Moltmann and Pannenberg but without documenting and arguing things in much detail.

Bultmann's view of the resurrection resembled that of Barth during the 1920's. It tended to merge the resurrection into revelation. Bultmann allowed the resurrection no independent status as a further event subsequent to the crucifixion and interpreted it as expressing the meaning of the cross.[15] Here again we meet the use of one model (revelation) in a way which rules out another (resurrection as history).

Moltmann's *Crucified God* alerts us to the fact that Jesus' death (together with his resurrection) forms the privileged place where the triune God stands revealed. There may be difficulties about the way Moltmann's trinitarian interpretation of the cross develops, but he has recalled a vital truth which for many Christians may be obscured by the long gap between Easter Sunday and the Feast of the Trinity. It is precisely in the paschal mystery that God is revealed as *triune*: the Father who "gave his Son up for us all" (Rom. 8:32), the Son who "became obedient unto death" (Phil. 2:8), and the Holy Spirit breathed into the world by the risen Son (Jn. 20:22).

Lastly, Pannenberg has attended notably to the revelatory dimension of the Lord's resurrection. His *Revelation as History* endorses the Hegelian view that nothing less than the whole of reality understood as history can disclose (indirectly) the divinity. Only the totality of history will supply the perspective from which we may grasp the entire course of history as the divine self-revelation. This totality has become available inasmuch as Christ's resurrection has *anticipated the end of all history*. With him there has already taken place what will happen for others at the end. For this model, the resurrection of Christ, while retaining its historical particularity, enjoys a uniquely absolute value in revealing God.

The Resurrection as Ground of Faith

The phenomenon of faith has provided the basic orientation for such writers on the resurrection as Gerhard Ebeling, Peter Selby and Willi Marxsen. An appendix to this book discusses in detail Marxsen's approach. Ebeling latches onto a prominent feature of the New Testament accounts: there are no Easter appearances without Easter faith.[16] During his ministry the many people who met and heard Jesus reacted in various ways: they hesitated to commit themselves, they turned hostile or they joined his disciples. It was different with the risen Christ. No one encountered the risen Lord without coming to faith or being reinforced in faith. Only a simplistic reading would take Paul's companions on the Damascus road in Acts and the Roman guards in Matthew as exceptions to this general affirmation.

Beyond question, there are difficulties to be noted in the way Ebeling handles the theme of faith. He almost makes the appearances of the risen Christ simply coincide with the disciples' coming to faith. Besides, he plays down the change brought by the crucifixion and resurrection. "The faith of the days after Easter," Ebeling declares, "knows itself to be nothing else but the right understanding of the Jesus of the days before Easter. . . . To believe in Jesus therefore means: to enter into relations with God in view of him, to let him give us the freedom to believe." The content of post-resurrection faith is not altered by "the additional fact of his resurrection." This faith is nothing else than "the consequence" of "the certainty of faith" shown by the historical Jesus.[17] The difficulties notwithstanding, Ebeling rightly draws our attention to a further interpretative model, the resurrection as grounding faith.

In his *Look for the Living* (properly subtitled *The Corporate Nature of Resurrection Faith*) Peter Selby skillfully develops this interpretative model. He clarifies both the "place" and the implications of Easter faith. "If it is resurrection that is being sought," he argues, "the communal must be the place of discovery." He finds "this communal dimension" lacking in "so many contemporary versions of the resurrection faith." Selby insists that, from the beginning, conversion "involved alliance with the new community just as much as it involved personal reorientation and the believing of the Easter story; it meant making one's own the life of a community, appropriating both its story and its values."[18] Like Ebeling, Selby orients his discussion of the resurrection toward faith. But unlike Ebeling and others, he appreciates deeply the community dimension of that faith. Selby also goes out of his way to define carefully what he means by the nature and content of faith.

The Resurrection as Ground of Hope

At the resurrection of Christ God reveals himself as the God who has raised and who will raise

the dead. The beginning of the end has arrived. The
new creation has begun. Here a further interpretative model for the resurrection swings into view—
the eschatological model. Christ's resurrection from
the dead communicates the final divine promise:
"Behold, I make all things new" (Rev. 21:5). That
promise points to the future and grounds our hopes
for human beings and their world.

Moltmann's classic *Theology of Hope* has
loomed large among attempts to interpret the resurrection as a promise which evokes hope. At times
the insights of his hope theology edged him toward a
one-sided emphasis. "The event of the raising of
Christ from the dead," he wrote, "is an event which
is understood *only* [italics mine] in the *modus* of
promise. It has its time still ahead of it, is grasped as
an 'historic phenomenon' *only* [italics mine] in its
relation to *its* future, and mediates to those who
know it a future toward which they have to move in
history."[19] However, even if such particular statements need to be nuanced, Moltmann's broad gen-
eralization proves convincing. The promise which
Easter Sunday holds out justifies us in recognizing
the theology of hope as offering a major interpretative key to the resurrection. *Spero ut intelligam
resurrectionem* (I hope in order that I might understand the resurrection).

One finds a similar perspective in *Gaudium et
Spes*, the *Pastoral Constitution on the Church in
the Modern World* issued by the Second Vatican
Council. In dealing with the paschal mystery, that
document recalls the hope held out to mankind and

all of creation through the Lord's rising from the dead:

> God is preparing a new dwelling and a new earth in which righteousness dwells, whose happiness will fill and surpass all the desires of peace arising in the hearts of men. Then with death conquered the sons of God will be raised in Christ and what was sown in weakness and dishonor will put on the imperishable: charity and its works will remain and all of creation, which God made for man, will be set free from its bondage to decay (n. 39).

The Resurrection as Ground of Kerygma

In the Easter narratives of Matthew, Luke and John everyone recognizes a missionary motif. The risen Lord encountered his disciples not to remain with them in a prolonged, ecstatic idyll but precisely to send them to announce the good news. In brief, the resurrection established the *kerygma*. Here we run up against a sixth interpretative model which we can reasonably associate with Bultmann. In this context he accepted a critic's formulation of his position: "Christ rose into the *kerygma*." Bultmann's language about proclamation is so emphatic that it hardly misrepresents his view if we speak of "the real presence of Christ in the *kerygma*." Bultmann fascinated and disconcerted two generations of exegetes and theologians. Time has not yet fully focused his contribution, but assuredly one point of lasting value will be his reminder that the mission to proclaim is a major model for interpreting the resurrection.

Looking back at the six models, I am painfully aware that my treatment has of necessity been tantalizingly brief. For instance, it may seem absurd to give only one paragraph to Bultmann and the kerygma. Nevertheless, this much can be said for attempting such rapid outlines. For those who know Bultmann's work, no longer account is necessary. For those who do not know his work, no relatively brief account is possible.

II
THE MODELS AND THEIR ORIGINS

So far this chapter has sketched six interpretative models which twentieth-century scholars have in fact used for interpreting Christ's resurrection. I shrink from leaving readers with the impression that a given theologian can or will be interested in only one such model. In fact, we have seen how Barth's interests led him to develop the models of history (1), redemption (2) and revelation (3), although his vast and wide-ranging writings include material which could have allowed us to list him also under faith (4), hope (5), and kerygma (6). Bultmann's name came up in connection with revelation (3) and kerygma (6) and Moltmann's in connection with revelation (3) and hope (5). Quite apart from specific instances of individual theologians using several models, it is obvious that the models naturally involve each other. To reflect deeply on the resurrection as historical reality inevitably raises the question: What kind of reality is it? An appropriate answer would be: It is a redemptive and revealing reality which both evokes faith and hope and should be proclaimed. The move from one model to another comes naturally.

The particular choice of models can be affected by *philosophical* concerns. When Moltmann read Ernst Bloch's *Das Prinzip Hoffnung (The Principle Hope)*, he drew from this humanist Marxist questions, concepts and language. These gave force and structure to his *Theology of Hope* and its central reflections on Christ's resurrection.[20] Those who live in Anglo-Saxon countries are likely to have their choice dictated by the perduring tradition of British empiricism and common sense. Discussions of the resurrection as an event of cosmic revelation and redemption may be brushed aside as fit only for continentals who hanker after the good old days of Hegelian idealism. Let us keep our feet on the ground and settle the historical facts. In some quarters the spirit of David Hume and others continues to maintain a philosophical climate in which theologians automatically choose model one (the resurrection as historical reality).

It may help readers to respond with more understanding and sympathy if I draw attention to three further features in my scheme of six models.

First, the models divide into two major groups.

Models one, two, and three concern the divine activity: the (historical) reality God has brought about *ante nos* and *extra nos*, the redemption effected *pro nobis*, and the revelation communicated to us. Models four, five and six focus on persons entering the community of Easter faith and hope which carries its message to the world. The first three models interpret matters in terms of the saving revelation effected through the event of Christ's resurrection. The last three models deal primarily with the human response to that saving and revealing event.

Secondly, we can see the models as developed in reply to six basic questions we can put when faced with some remarkable story. Three of these questions are borrowed from Immanuel Kant ("What can I know? What ought I to do? What may I hope for?"). The first model forms in response to the question: "What can I know?" If I use my powers of human understanding and check the Easter story, what can I conclude about the historical truth? Secondly, lostness, suffering and sin plague and oppress our human situation. How does Christ's resurrection help and save us? How can it cope with our felt need for redemption?

The third model of the resurrection grows out of the questions: How does God speak to us through the events of Good Friday and Easter Sunday? What was being revealed there? The fourth question touches our self-understanding: How do we interpret our lives and commit ourselves when faced with the Lord's resurrection? Kant's "What may I hope for?" can serve to introduce the fifth model. The last model takes its cue from Kant's "What ought I to do?'' In the context of the resurrection this question becomes: What good news ought I to carry to others?

These six questions indicate the mindsets of various theologians when dealing with the resurrection. To appreciate why they developed various interpretative models it helps to identify the basic question(s) they sought to answer when they spoke of the resurrection. It may have been better to have purged Kant's questions of their blatant individualism and asked: ''What can we know? What ought we to do? What may we hope for?'' However I decided to leave the questions in their original form.

The last feature to be noted in the scheme of six interpretative models is its foundation in the New Testament. What Selby has termed ''the pluriformity of the resurrection proclamation in the New Testament'' provides the basis for the plurality of interpretative models. Just as in the New Testament ''the offering of a single interpretation'' of the resurrection was ''out of the question,'' so we should not expect contemporary Church teaching and theology to come up with some *single* and coherent account of what the mystery of the resurrection is. To echo Selby, both at the beginning of Christianity and now no *single* statement or model ''would faithfully present the resurrection faith.''[21]

We can quickly cite some New Testament texts to illustrate that pluriformity which prepares the way for the later pluriformity of interpretative models.

(1) Embedded in the Emmaus story we find

what looks like an early formulation recalling Peter's priority as Easter witness: "The Lord has risen indeed, and has appeared to Simon" (Lk. 24:34). In this memorably concise statement a major emphasis lies on the facts of the resurrection and the appearance to Peter. To be sure, it is no "mere historical" report. "Lord," "risen," and "appear" are words packed with theological meaning and implications. Nevertheless, the statement heavily stresses the *reality* of the resurrection and subsequent appearance, without adding interpretations and indicating the consequences of Easter. We do not read: "The Lord has risen indeed for our justification and as the first fruits of those who have fallen asleep. He has appeared to tell Simon to make disciples of all nations." Passages like Luke 24:34 serve as scriptural starting points for developing the interpretative model of the resurrection as historical reality.

(2) We do not have to search far in the New Testament to find the resurrection being understood as *redemptive*. Christ was "raised for our justification" (Rom. 4:25) and "became a life-giving spirit" (2 Cor. 15:45). Redemptive interpretations of the Lord's rising from the dead abound in Paul's letters, to which we can add the fact that John, Luke and Paul—albeit in somewhat different ways—all link the saving and sanctifying gift of the Holy Spirit to the death and resurrection of Christ.

(3) In Galatians Paul reaches for the theme of *revelation* to interpret what happened to him in his encounter with the risen Christ. He speaks of his

''Gospel'' coming ''through a revelation of Jesus Christ.'' For God ''was pleased to reveal his Son'' to Paul (Gal. 1:12 and 16). The revelatory significance of Easter shows up elsewhere in the New Testament—when, for instance, the risen Christ opened his disciples' ''minds to understand the Scriptures'' (Lk. 24:27 and 45).

(4) Paul has provided the classic text for associating resurrection and *faith*: ''If Christ has not been raised, your faith is futile'' (1 Cor. 15:17). John chooses nothing other than the theme of Easter faith for the climax of his Gospel. The risen Jesus says to Thomas: ''Have you believed because you have seen me? Blessed are those who have not seen and yet believe'' (Jn. 20:29).

(5) 1 Corinthians 15 celebrates vividly the *hope* communicated through the Lord's resurrection. The power of death will disintegrate. The promise of Easter is clear: ''As in Adam all die, so also in Christ shall all be made alive'' (1 Cor. 15:22).

(6) Finally, we can easily appeal to Paul and Matthew for passages interpreting the resurrection as initiating *proclamation*. Paul explains that the Damascus road encounter took place with a view to mission among the Gentiles (Gal. 1:16). His apostolic vocation relates to his being a witness to the risen Lord: ''Am I not an apostle? Have I not seen Christ our Lord?'' (1 Cor. 9:1).

This sampling of New Testament texts should illustrate that Klappert's work is more than just another artifact of the German theological industry. In this chapter I have tried to build on his initial thoughts to show how both contemporary theology and the New Testament support the same thesis. The resurrection of Christ calls for a pluriformity of converging interpretative models. Provided we do not attempt to absolutize one model and make it our exclusive means for interpreting Easter, we will find that the models turn out to be happily complementary rather than distressingly contradictory.

After pursuing the convergences in resurrection theology, we turn in the next chapter to certain questions that continue to produce genuinely irreconcilable positions.

2
Questions

In his *Reason, Truth and God,* Renford Bambrough sums up Matthew Arnold's version of Christianity thus:

> What he does say is that what is usually
> thought to be meant by the propositions of the
> Christian religion is unverified and unverifi-
> able, and that therefore those propositions
> must mean something else that he *can* believe.
> This is a gross *non sequitur*, but it is not a rare
> aberration, not an idiosyncratic lapse on the
> part of Arnold. It is a common response to the
> predicament that Arnold found himself in.[1]

What Arnold (1822-1888) did with the propositions of the Christian religion in general has often
been done with the specific New Testament propositions about Jesus' resurrection. Rather than what
they appear to mean, these propositions must mean
something which *can* be believed—something less
than a personal resurrection for Jesus himself. I call
this response underbelief. With it I want to discuss
the phenomenon of overbelief, the tendency (at

41

times blatantly fundamentalistic) to interpret literally all the physical details we find in the Easter narratives, especially those of Luke and John.

This chapter will then consider two related questions. What light does the New Testament throw upon the *experience* of the risen Christ which believers now enjoy? In what ways should we "watch our language" about the resurrection of the Lord?

Underbelief

With Christ's resurrection the temptation to act like Arnold and underinterpret the meaning of New Testament propositions is at its strongest. The result of such a reduction may be a meaning that is believable, but it will be one that fails to match what the original texts wanted to communicate.

Generally underinterpretation takes the form of reading the New Testament proclamation "Jesus is risen" as no more than an expression of the disciples' inner life. They became convinced of the value to be found in Jesus' message and example. The miracle of belief happened. They spoke and wrote of his "resurrection," but this was only a way of talking about the rise of their faith. The disciples meant to communicate what happened to them, not what happened to Jesus. They wanted to articulate their newly-found moral commitments, not make factual claims about the fate of Jesus after Good Friday. In *The Resurrection of Jesus Christ* I described this reductionist version of the Easter texts as follows:

> When Paul and the other witnesses claimed to have encountered Jesus alive after his death, they really meant: "His words came alive for us, God's grace helped us to see the truth of his cause, and with the divine help we intend to continue his mission." In these terms the stories of the resurrection appearances simply form concrete, pictorial descriptions of changed convictions. Before his crucifixion the disciples had heard Jesus' words on which they reflected in the light of his death. Their outlook changed, so that they decided to accept fully his message. Essentially, their Easter proclamation amounted to (1) the affirmation of some general principle(s) (for instance, "love conquers"), which they expressed through symbolic narratives ("God raised Jesus from the dead"), and (2) an invitation to lead a life in accordance with these principles (p. 32).

In *The Resurrection of Jesus Christ* I indicated ways in which Paul van Buren and Lloyd Geering represent such possibilities for underinterpreting the Easter texts in the New Testament. The appendix to this little book shows how Marxsen is more or less comfortable about reducing resurrection-talk to the "miraculous" emergence of faith—first Peter's faith and then that of other disciples.

Here we can spot the startling difference be-

tween the reductionists and "traditional" skeptics
and rationalists like David Hume. The rationalists
accepted the *meaning* of the New Testament texts,
but in the name of reason and common sense rejected the *truth* of Christ's resurrection. The reductionists, however, alter the meaning of the texts and
then accept the truth they have fashioned for themselves.

Selby brings to bear a decisive argument
against underinterpretations which allege that
"speaking of the resurrection of Jesus was a way of
using the cultural furniture of the age to express the
truth of faith." Choosing resurrection language for
such a purpose would have been extraordinarily
odd. It would have caused "the maximum confusion" to Jewish audiences and been incomprehen-
sible to Gentile audiences. We can safely maintain
with Selby at least this minimum. It is hardly "unreasonable" to suppose that in proclaiming the resurrection the early Christians were affirming
"something to do with Jesus."[2]

Selby attends here to the *proclamation* of the
first Christians. In his recent review of a collection
of essays on Mark 14—16 (which tend both to underinterpret and misinterpret), Raymond Brown
makes a similar point apropos of the biblical *texts*
and *authors*. Challenging the (essentially reductionist) interpretations which several essays offer of
Mark's account of the Last Supper, Peter's role and
Christ's resurrection, he puts his finger on the key
difficulty that repeatedly confronts such underinterpretations: "If these four essays are right, Mark

was one of the most incompetent writers of all times, since almost all his readers have interpreted him to say the opposite of what he intended about the Eucharist, about Peter and about the resurrection."[3]

The Selby-Brown argument finds support from linguistic philosophy. P. F. Strawson remarks that "we may expect a certain regularity of relationship between what people intend to communicate by uttering certain sentences and what those sentences conventionally mean."[4] Even when (as often happens) a speaker or writer does not formulate explicitly his intentions, nevertheless the content, general usage and public conventions governing the recognition of words normally indicate what he or she wishes to convey. We would normally require strong evidence before agreeing that some statements express a hidden meaning which differs from their conventional sense. A serious prior disposition on our side to find a more believable meaning hardly excuses us from dispensing with such evidence when we feel under pressure to allege such a hidden meaning.

In the case of the New Testament, not only the context of late Judaism but also the general usage of biblical literature and the conventions governing the recognition of words should lead us to conclude that the writers meant just what their words about Jesus' resurrection said. God had intervened to rescue him from death. In a new and glorious existence Jesus presented himself alive to those who had known him to die by crucifixion. The New Testament authors used resurrection language primarily to affirm such a truth about Jesus. If they had wanted to write primarily about the rise of their faith, they could have done just that. Appropriate words were available. "Faith" *(pistis)*, "to believe" *(pisteuein)* and their synonyms are among the commonest words in the New Testament. *Pistis* turns up 243 times and *pisteuein* 241 times.

Overbelief

Underinterpretation and underbelief may be common responses to the kind of predicament in which Matthew Arnold found himself. However, an even more frequent response seems to be what I call "overbelief," the mistaken decision to interpret as strictly "accurate" all the details in the Easter narratives. This means more than simply insisting that the risen Christ actually uttered every one of the words attributed to him by Matthew, Luke, John and the appendix to Mark (16:9-20). Such overbelief also entails holding that he quite literally took and ate a piece of broiled fish (Lk. 24:42f.), and that more or less gaping holes remained in the hands and side of his risen body (Jn. 20:20, 25, 27).

It is easy to spot the weak and even comic side of such overinterpretations. If a resurrected man took a snack, what kind of digestive system did his body have? Can ordinary food be transformed into glorious (normally invisible?) matter or does it pass through without genuinely interacting with such a

body? And how could five wounds (the nail marks
in hands and feet, as well as the lance wound in the
side) remain in this body? Several years ago I found
myself—to my discredit—noisily demanding of an
archbishop: "What kind of a risen body do you
imagine Christ to have if it still has a gaping hole in
its side?" Excessively realistic interpretations of
the Easter texts in Luke and John logically lead to
pseudo-problems like the digestive capacity of a
risen body, or the failure of the disciples on the
Emmaus road to notice that the stranger had holes
in his hands and feet. Such misinterpretations of the
resurrection resemble D. H. Lawrence's version in
The Man Who Died. In that short novel Christ rises
numb, cold, torn and "full of hurt." He creeps out
of the tomb "with the caution of the bitterly
wounded." His "hurt feet" touch the earth again,
"with unspeakable pain." This portrayal of the resurrection degrades it not only to the resuscitation of
a corpse but even to one which fails to restore the
corpse to the full bodily integrity possessed before
the execution took place.

What lurks behind the phenomenon of overin-
terpretation is often the influence of art. The next
chapter will argue that the artistic imagination can
properly contribute to our appreciation of the resurrection. But here I wish to note a specific weakness
in much Western painting and sculpture that has
taken as its subject the risen Christ. Undoubtedly a
few artists coped as successfully as one might expect: Piero della Francesca, El Greco and—
perhaps the best of all—Grünewald with his radiant

Christ rising against a midnight sky. However, others presented the risen Lord in ways that blur the distinction between resurrection and mere reanimation. I think here especially of those many representations of the doubting Thomas. Caravaggio, Donatello and other artists show the apostle about to insert his finger in the wounded side of Christ. The craving for the tangible and the concern for proof overlay and smother the sense that the resurrection took the Lord into a new final and glorious state of existence.

The proper interpretation of the Easter narratives calls for a critical, not an exaggerated, realism. Such an approach *both* evaluates Luke and John in the light of other New Testament texts concerned with resurrection, *and* also seeks to appreciate the intentions of the evangelists themselves. Let me develop these points. My aim is to make it clear to readers why I draw the line between excessive realism and critical realism at the precise points that I do.

First of all, it would be an awesome evasion to deal with the Lucan and Johannine ''realism'' in isolation from the rest of the New Testament. On the one hand, in Luke's narrative the risen Christ walks a road for several hours, sits at table, invites others to handle him, and eats fish to persuade his disciples that he is no ghost (Lk. 24:15ff. 39-43). In John's story he shows his disciples his hands and his side, and invites them to touch his risen body in which the marks of the wounds still remain (Jn. 20:20-27). On the other hand, however, Paul's reflections in 1 Corinthians 15 convey no suggestion that the risen Jesus has returned to any kind of "earthly" existence and activities. Raised and exalted to heaven, Christ emerges from his invisible state to encounter some privileged witnesses. His body is "spiritual," not "physical." "Flesh and blood," Paul declares roundly, "cannot inherit the kingdom of heaven" (1 Cor. 15:44, 50). Paul's notion of transformation through resurrection challenges and criticizes the picture of physical reanimation that the third and fourth Gospels seem to offer. In a debate with some Sadducees Jesus likewise denies that resurrection means a return to the existence and activities of this world (Mk. 12:24-27). He indicates that risen life will be a glorious, "angelic" state (Mt. 13:43). By insisting on the strict accuracy of the physical details in the Easter narratives of Luke and John, we will flatly contradict the understanding of resurrection proposed by Jesus and Paul. But do we have to produce such an interpretation of Luke and John?

Those two Gospel writers allow us to detect both the *motivation* for their vivid, corporeal emphasis and their own way of *qualifying* this. The physical detail is there not so much to tell us about the nature of Jesus' glorious body, but to highlight three points: (a) the reality of the resurrection, (b) the continuity between the risen Lord and the earthly Jesus, and (c) the disciples' status as witnesses. Jesus truly rose from the dead as a total human being. It was no mere ghost or spirit that encountered the disciples. He presented himself as identical with the Jesus who had lived and died: "It is I myself" (Lk. 24:39). His followers recognized him as such (Lk. 24:31; Jn. 20:16; 21:7. 12). The graphic, physical touches of the Easter stories in Luke and John serve to express these points and no more. It would be a mistake to press them further, as if they were reporting visible detail that a camera and/or a tape recorder could have preserved for us.

Moreover, Luke and John apparently realize that their "realistic" emphasis could seem to imply that the Lord's resurrection was no more than the resuscitation of a corpse. To head off such a misunderstanding they qualify their presentation by including details which indicate the transformed existence of the risen Lord. He passes through closed doors (Jn. 20:19. 26). He suddenly appears and disappears (Lk. 24:31-36). He leaves his followers by ascending into the sky (Acts 1:9). A recurrent motif in Luke and John also suggests the transformation brought by resurrection. People who had known the earthly Jesus fail, at least initially, to identify the risen Lord. On the road to Emmaus the two disciples recognize him only in the moment of his disappearance (Lk. 24:31). Mary Magdalene supposes him to be a gardener (Jn. 20:14f.). At the end of their night's fishing Peter and his companions do not at once identify the stranger who stands on the shore (Jn. 21:4ff.). In *The Resurrection of Jesus Christ* I summed up the approach of the third and fourth evangelists this way:

In a low key both Luke and John call our attention to the transformation involved in Christ's resurrection. If they emphasize his *physical* presence to counter "spiritualizing" aberrations, they also allow for a certain "heavenly otherness" to prevent crassly materialistic views which would reduce the resurrection to the reanimation of a corpse (pp. 84f.).

In short, the interpretation of Luke and John demands a "critical realism." Such an interpretation picks its way between two extremes: the reductionism of underbelief which denies the reality of the resurrection, and the literalism of an overbelief which woodenly takes certain vivid details to be strictly "accurate" and thereby misses their true function in the stories. Critical realism avoids both the prejudice of the reductionists ("The New Testament texts about Christ's resurrection can't possibly mean what they seem to mean"), and the fears of the literalists ("Where will such interpretation all stop?").

Before leaving "overbelief" in the resurrection stories, we need to come to grips with a further question that might occur to the reader. Did the risen Lord actually utter the words attributed to him by Matthew, Luke and John?[5] Would it make any real difference if we decided that these words were all formulated later—either personally by the Gospel writers themselves or by the Christian traditions on which they drew?

Severe biblical and doctrinal worries can flare up for some Christians when faced with such questions. The reliability of the Gospels and the divine institution of the sacraments (or at least of baptism) seem threatened. If the post-resurrection sayings of Jesus were all created by the early Church traditions or by the evangelists, how could we hold that the Gospels accurately report his preaching prior to his death? The Great Commission at the end of Matthew (together with the Last Supper narratives) guarantees—at least for baptism and the Eucharist—the truth on which the Council of Trent insisted: Christ, and not the Church, instituted the sacraments.

Many theologians have made their peace with the second problem. In founding the Church, which is the primordial sacrament, Christ instituted the sacraments. There is no doctrinal need to maintain that the command to baptize must as such be historically authentic—in the sense of deriving literally from the mouth of the risen Lord.

But what of the general issue of reliability? Where will it all stop if we doubt the authenticity of the risen Christ's words? A number of considerations, however, suggest how such a worry is unfounded.

(a) Assuming that the Gospels—or at least Matthew, Mark and Luke—are substantially reliable in reporting Jesus' words during his ministry, we may not without further ado suppose then that the brief stories concerned with the risen Lord necessarily exhibit at all points the same historical reliability. We dare not overlook the drastic transformation between the *ante-mortem* and the *post-*

mortem states of Jesus. To report what he said during his earthly existence evidently differs radically from reporting what he said when he moved into his final state of glorified life.

(b) In fact, the words of the risen Lord in any one Gospel are only approximately paralleled in other Gospels. A quick comparison between the final words of Jesus in the various Gospels (Mt. 28:18-20; Lk. 24:47-49 and Jn. 20:21-23) shows how much the wording differs. In these Easter texts we find nothing like the close and extensive parallelisms between sayings reported from the ministry of Jesus.

(c) An obvious historical problem arises from the fact that Matthew, Luke and John represent the risen Lord as explicitly setting in motion a universal mission. However, if he had given such a clear command to evangelize the world, how can we explain the evidence from Chapters 10 and 15 of Acts—not to mention the letters of Paul? There decisions are taken to engage in such a mission, but *not* on the basis of recalling and obeying the risen Lord's explicit instructions.

(d) A final consideration: The style of the risen Lord's language reflects clearly the characteristics of particular evangelists. Matthew, for instance, ends his Gospel with what looks very much like his own construction: "All authority in heaven and earth has been given to me. Go therefore and make disciples of all nations, baptizing them in the name of the Father and of the Son and of the Holy Spirit, teaching them to observe all that I have commanded you; and lo, I am with you always to the close of the age." These words recall language and summarize themes of the first Gospel in a way which makes the section "a climax and conclusion of Matthew's particular presentation of the Gospel material and of the figure of Christ, and which would make it as out of place at the end of any other Gospel as it is completely in place here."[6] The passage contains several very characteristic Matthean motifs: "making disciples," the teaching aspect of the Church's mission, and Jesus' function in communicating the new law.

To sum up: There are good reasons for doubting that the risen Lord literally spoke the words attributed to him in Matthew, Luke and John. However, this is *not* to call into question, and certainly not to deny, the high importance of Matthew's Great Commission and other such post-Easter texts. At the very least they express part of the true significance which the early Christians acknowledged in the resurrection itself and in the encounters with the risen Christ. Moreover, we could well speak of "some type of intuitive communication by Jesus that found words later in the various traditions." In that sense, we could envisage "a general missionary mandate that was subsequently formulated differently in the different Gospel traditions."[7] Such a solution respects the obvious divergences between the sayings in the Easter narratives, while recognizing the context to which all these sayings point: the encounters with the risen Lord. These encounters conveyed a call to mission. The followers of the Lord *heard* him—not in the

sense of picking up vocalized words transmitted
through sound waves, but in the sense of knowing
his presence and feeling driven joyfully and obe-
diently to proclaim him as vindicated and victori-
ous. In that respect their experience of the risen
Christ is to be compared not so much with their
experience of the historical Jesus during his preaching, but rather with the Old Testament prophets
who "heard" God. Those prophets did not literally
listen to words ringing out from heaven. At times,
however, they experienced some kind of over-
whelming presence of God which drove them to
announce—in their own images and terminology—
the divine message of comfort, rebuke, prediction
and so forth.

In general we would do well to respect the
analogy between the Old Testament theophanies
and the appearances of the risen Christ. Through his
resurrection he "lives now to God" (Rom. 6:10)—
not in the sense of his humanity being annihilated
but of its being taken into the divine sphere. When
the risen Lord appears, he does so as one whose
human existence has been glorified and divinized as
fully as that is possible. This truth could encourage
us to speak of Christophanies rather than simply of
appearances.

Present Experience

So far in this chapter we have looked at two
tendencies which continue to set questions going
about the resurrection of Jesus and the Easter

stories in the New Testament: the tendency to underbelief and the (opposing) fundamentalist tendency to overbelief. Both these tendencies concern
directly what happened in the *past* — "back there"
and "back then." But what of *present* belief and
experience? Here again we bump up against two
opposite tendencies. Some presume that they can in
no way share the experience of Mary Magdalene,
Peter and the others who encountered the risen and
glorious Lord. Others argue that their experience of
the Lord exactly matches that of the first Christians
in the days following the resurrection. In short,
there can be both underbelief and overbelief as regards our present experience of the risen Christ.

First of all, let us consider underbelief. Many
people, I suspect, can study the Easter narratives in
Luke and John, finish up with notebooks bulging
with biblical comments and theological facts, but
never manage to identify themselves with Mary
Magdalene, Thomas, Cleopas or the other disciple
on the Emmaus road. They are missing something
highly important. The enduring experience of the
Lord forms a centerpiece in the way Luke and John
present the resurrection. These two Gospel writers
point to the Eucharist, the reading of Scripture, the
forgiveness of sins, the confession of faith and other
elements in Church life which signal the continuing
presence of the risen Christ. Through their personal
faith later Christians can enjoy an intimate relationship with the Lord. In that, they resemble the
founding fathers and founding mothers of the
Church who experienced him in those days immediately after his resurrection.

This later entering into that basic experience is clearly expressed in Luke's Emmaus story (Lk. 24:13-35). The risen Jesus is understood to speak when the Scriptures are read and explained in the Christian liturgy. He kindles faith and makes hearts burn with the desire to meet him more intimately in the Eucharist. It is precisely when minds are opened to the Scriptures and hearts are moved to faith that people are ready to encounter him in the sacrament. The readings from the Bible prepare the way for the Lord who makes himself present in the breaking of the bread. In the Emmaus story Luke evidently intends to relate the Christian experience of the Eucharist to the experience of those men and women who encountered Christ radiantly alive after his death. More than this, Luke's story hints at something larger than the liturgical assembly—that life's journey in which we search for the Lord and in which he comes to us. In an unpublished paper Philip O'Reilly put it this way: "The Emmaus narrative describes two pilgrims' progress to their encounter with the risen Lord. Their journey is representative, because it is the journey of every Christian who has not seen Jesus in his risen body."

Léon-Dufour and others have drawn attention to the parallel between the Emmaus story and the meeting of Philip the deacon with the Ethiopian eunuch in Acts 8:26-39. That episode too concerns a journey. This journey symbolizes a search. The search ends with the eunuch finding the key to Scriptures, coming to know Jesus and receiving baptism. Léon-Dufour concludes: "It is clear that, in these two episodes, Luke is showing the reader what the behavior of a Christian must be: it is in baptism and the Eucharist that contact with Jesus Christ takes place."[8]

Are there any limits to be observed here? Can we identify the encounters between the risen Christ and the original witnesses as being totally the same as the experiences of the Lord enjoyed by later Christians—or, for that matter, as being totally the same as the knowing of Christ in faith which those very witnesses subsequently had? John Macquarrie answers in the affirmative. Apropos of the meeting with the risen Christ which Paul reports in 1 Corinthians 15:8, he observes: "It is not unreasonable to suppose that it is . . . on a par with the encounters which subsequent believers may have had with the risen Christ."[9] Louis Evely flatly asserts: "The apparitions of which the apostles speak are apparitions that we ourselves can experience."[10] Macquarrie, Evely and others indulge overbelief here. There was not and is not such an absolute democracy of experience in our access to the risen Christ.

The difference revolves around two themes, identification and mission. Peter, Mary Magdalene, Thomas and others recognize the risen Christ as being identical with the master whom they have known and followed. The beloved disciple identifies the stranger on the beach: "It is the Lord" (Jn. 21:7). No later group or person—not even St. Paul—can duplicate this aspect of those first postresurrection meetings with Christ. Only those who have known him during his earthly ministry can acknowledge the risen Lord in his final glory to be one and the same person as Jesus of Nazareth. Peter, Mary Magdalene, Cleopas and other disciples serve as bridge people who link the period of Jesus' ministry with the post-Easter situation. In that way their experience of the risen Lord is unique and irrepeatable.

Secondly, Peter, Paul and other apostolic witnesses who meet the risen Christ have the *mission* to testify to that experience and found the Church. These witnesses have seen for themselves and believed. In proclaiming the good news and gathering together those who have not seen and yet are ready to believe, these original witnesses do not need to rely on the experience and testimony of others. Their function for Christianity differs from that of any subsequent believers, inasmuch as they alone have the once-and-for-all task of inaugurating the mission and founding the Church. Others will bear the responsibility to continue that mission and keep the Church in existence. But the coming-into-being of the mission and of the Church cannot be duplicated. The way in which that unique function rests upon some (ontological) difference in experience is expressed by John's classic distinction between those who have seen and believed and those who are "blessed" because they "have not seen and yet believe" (Jn. 20:29).

St. Paul also draws attention to some difference between the fundamental post-resurrection encounters and all later experiences of the risen Lord. "Last of all," he recalls, Christ "appeared also to me" (1 Cor. 15:8). This episode constituted Paul's apostolic calling and the basis for his mission (1 Cor. 9:1; Gal. 1:11ff.). Other Christians share with him the gift of the Holy Spirit and life "in Christ," but they do not experience that fundamental meeting with the risen Lord which made Paul a founding father of the Church. He never remarks to his readers, "Christ appeared" or "Christ will appear to you." Furthermore, Paul claims to have received later ecstatic experiences, "visions and revelations of the Lord" (2 Cor. 12:1ff.), but he does not argue that they validate his fundamental role as apostolic witness to the resurrection. Even in the case of Paul such experiences differ from that basic encounter which made him the apostle to the Gentiles. If Paul distinguishes such occurrences in his own life from the encounters listed in 1 Corinthians 15:5-8, this distinction holds true all the more of any experiences which later believers will have of the risen Lord.

The Language of the Resurrection

Finally we reach the question: How should we speak about the risen Lord? What are the right ways here to use the language of faith? Some may dismiss terminological discussions as a triviality which threatens to claim and waste our time. However, poorly chosen and poorly used language has never helped people, especially when dealing with the mystery of Christ's resurrection.

The language question often circles around

pairs of words: spiritual and physical, objective and subjective, resurrection and life, and resurrection and exaltation. We need to observe the possibilities here, so that muddied usage does not obscure our answer to the question: What happened to Jesus after his death?

It takes no great effort to pry loose highly divergent ways of taking up "spiritual" and "physical." It is evident that "spiritual" could be employed in some weak and unacceptable sense: Jesus lives on "spiritually" in the devotion and commitment of his followers. At the same time, one could join Paul in speaking of a "spiritual body" (1 Cor. 15:44). Through his resurrection Jesus was transformed into a spirit-filled existence and became "a life-giving spirit" (1 Cor. 15:45). "Physical" is likewise an ambiguous word here. One person may choose the term as little more than the means of insisting that the resurrection truly took place. Another may speak of a physical resurrection in a way that reduces it to the mere resuscitation of a corpse. The soul of Jesus left his body and then returned to it like someone going out of the house at night and coming back in the morning. It is something of a shock to hear such an "explanation" of the resurrection, which simply ignores the transformation and glorification stressed by Paul in 1 Corinthians. All in all, the term "physical" seems peculiarly prone to encourage misinterpretations of the resurrection as mere reanimation. Hence I prefer to speak of "bodily" resurrection. This term is less open to such misinterpretations.

N B.

"Objective" and "subjective" are a notoriously tricky pair. It is one thing to call the resurrection objective in the sense of its being "there" in reality, prior to and independent of faith and not as the mere projection of some pressing subjective need. It is quite another thing to slip into portraying the Lord's resurrection as if it were a neutral event, available for acceptance by some uncommitted observer. His resurrection was not to be known in such a way by a disinterested spectator. Nor were his appearances "objective" in the sense that they could have been seen and recorded by a curious Roman tourist like a Pliny the Elder wanting to observe the eruption of Vesuvius.

The alternative of "resurrection" or "life" is firmly rooted in New Testament usage. St. Paul normally speaks of resurrection and only occasionally uses "life" or "living" with reference to the risen Christ: "The death he died he died to sin, once for all, but the life he lives he lives to God" (Rom. 6:10; see Rom. 14:9 and Gal. 2:20). However, it is Luke who popularizes the language of life, although without absolutely sacrificing the terminology of resurrection. At the empty tomb the women were asked: "Why do you seek the living among the dead?" (Lk. 24:5). Before his ascension Jesus frequently "presented himself alive"(Acts 1:3). The Roman governor Festus explained to King Agrippa how Paul asserted that Jesus was "alive" (Acts 25:19). "Resurrection" and "life" form a sequence. Life was and is the reality which resulted from the original act of resurrection. In his Easter broadcast of 1977 Pope Paul VI adopted these terms to indicate precisely that sequence: "Christ is risen; Christ lives." Paul's language of resurrection and Luke's language can be brought together in that way.

Finally, it would be evasive to raise the issue of language without tackling that classic pair, resurrection and exaltation. On the one hand, no treatment should command ready acceptance unless it frankly admits that resurrection language by itself does not suffice to convey the full meaning of what happened to Jesus after his death. Such language "is singularly lacking in the imagery of glory,"[11] whereas exaltation language is the idiom par excellence that expresses the glory and beauty of the post-Easter Lord (1 Tim. 3:16). On the other hand, resurrection (and not exaltation) language became normative in the Church's creeds. It was required, in order to differentiate the fate of Jesus from other possibilities—for instance, from that of one Old Testament figure to whom he was at times linked (Mk. 9:4ff.; 15:34ff.). Without dying, the prophet Elijah was, according to the legend, taken up into heaven by a fiery chariot. What happened to Jesus involved a death and needed to be stated more specifically than the term "exaltation" could manage. A resurrection is always an exaltation. Elijah's case illustrates that not all exaltations are resurrections.

Passages from two of Paul's letters can serve to elucidate the relationship between resurrection and exaltation language. 1 Corinthians 15:3-5 reads:

> I delivered to you as of first importance what I also received, that Christ died for our sins in accordance with the Scriptures, that he was

buried, that he was *raised* on the third day in accordance with the Scriptures, and that he appeared to Cephas [=Peter], then to the Twelve.

Philippians 2, 5-9 runs as follows:

Though he [Christ Jesus] was in the form of God,
he did not count equality with God
a thing to be grasped,
but emptied himself,
taking the form of a servant,
being born in the likeness of men.
And being found in human form
he humbled himself
and became obedient unto death,
even death of a cross.
Therefore God has *highly exalted* him
and bestowed on him the name
which is above every name,
that at the name of Jesus
every knee should bow,
in heaven and on earth and under the earth,
and every tongue should confess
that Jesus Christ is Lord,
to the glory of God the Father.

At least three major differences concerning resurrection and exaltation language emerge from a comparison between these two passages.

(a) In 1 Corinthians Paul cites a *creedal confession*. Both here and elsewhere (for instance,

Romans 10:9) resurrection language belongs to such brief confessions of faith. The language of exaltation, however, is found in early Christian *hymns* like Philippians 2:6ff. or 1 Timothy 3:16. The literary setting for resurrection and exaltation language differs.

(b) There is a "before" and "after" to resurrection language. It is more "horizontal." The one who was raised had previously died. Such language links God's action with history and time. As Selby remarks, "the stories of the resurrection of Jesus point both backward to the Jesus of the ministry and the death, and forward to the fulfillment of God's purpose which the raising of Jesus had anticipated."[12] One should also note how resurrection talk, as in 1 Corinthians 15, indicates that after being "raised on the third day" the Lord appeared to certain individuals and groups who existed within the conditions of normal human history. They could identify him as continuous with the Jesus of Nazareth who had lived, preached and been executed.

The hymnic language of exaltation, however, is the language of "up" and "down"—or rather of "down" and "up." It is more "vertical." The one who is below is taken into some higher sphere. This language tends to prescind from time and history. In Philippians the exalted Lord does not appear to human beings on a Damascus road, outside the tomb or at any other stated point in space and time. In such exaltation passages neither individuals (like Mary Magdalene or Peter) nor groups (like the

Twelve) have the function of identifying the Lord as being the same person as the master whom they followed during his ministry. In the hymn from Philippians, if "the name" of the exalted Jesus causes "every knee" to bow, these are knees "in heaven" and "under the earth," as well as "on earth."

(c) Third, resurrection and exaltation also differ inasmuch as resurrection language highlights the saving value and consequences "for us" *(pro nobis)* of Good Friday and Easter Sunday. To cite a traditional formula used by Paul: "Jesus was put to death for our trespasses and raised for our justification" (Rom. 4:25). Exaltation language, however, concentrates on Jesus' own transformation, that glorification through which he became Lord of the universe. Exaltation is primarily something "for Christ" himself *(pro Christo)*.

One could continue spinning out niceties here. For instance, resurrection language seems more eschatological than exaltation language. It deals with the end that lies ahead for human beings and their world. The exaltation language of Philippians 2:6-11, 1 Timothy 3:16 and other passages, however, does not as such lead us on clearly to the *eschaton*. One could also move beyond resurrection-exaltation language to examine other pairs of words like historical and transhistorical (or metahistorical). It could also be rewarding to confront the weak sense in which Lloyd Geering applies "symbol" and "symbolic" to the resurrection with the strong sense that R. C. Ware attaches to that term.

This treatment of the language to be used in regard to Christ's resurrection has done little more than sample certain points. Such language has often fallen into careless hands. It has never become the theme of such serious debates as led to Church councils and produced classic formulations about the person of Christ. At no time has the "right" language for the resurrection involved the whole Church in controversy and reflection. Hence the sloppy use of terminology here may be understandable, but it is never excusable.

This chapter has picked apart and chewed over several questions about the resurrection which repeatedly arise either at the popular or at the scholarly level. In the next two chapters we turn to some themes which promise to be growth points for those who reflect on Christ's resurrection. We take up first the role of the imagination.

3
The Imagination and the Resurrection

"Nothing," David Hume maintained, "is more dangerous to reason than flights of the imagination, and nothing has been the occasion of more mistakes among philosophers."[1] Hume has hardly proved the most popular philosopher in Christian circles. Nevertheless, ever since the era of the Church Fathers many theologians have done their work as if nothing were more dangerous to theological reason than flights of the imagination.

To cite one recent example. In his *On Being a Christian* (New York, 1976), Hans Küng insists that resurrection involves "a radical transformation into a wholly different state." The "reality of the resurrection" is "completely *intangible* and *unimaginable*." Like Hume he warns against letting the imagination cause mistakes: "Neither sight nor the imagination can help us here; they can only mislead us" (p. 350).

Undoubtedly the imagination can lead us at times into a mess. That happens when we use images in misguided attempts to describe and explain other-worldly realities. This is probably what Küng wishes to warn his readers against. At the same time, could there be value in the view championed by the romantics—that art and the imagination provide an authentic way of reaching reality? Keats put his conviction clearly: "What the imagination seizes as beauty must be truth." More than two centuries before that Shakespeare made Theseus declare in *A Midsummer Night's Dream* (Act V, Scene I):

> Lovers and madmen have such seething brains,
> Such shaping fantasies, that apprehend
> More than cool reason ever comprehends.
> The lunatic, the lover and the poet
> Are of imagination all compact.

To Shakespeare's lunatics, lovers and poets we can add artists, actors and children among those who can favor the imagination rather than the mind.

What then of Christ's resurrection and our imagination? Can we let some images prompt useful intuitions, provided we check any impulse to indulge bizarre efforts at describing precisely what risen life would look like? If we refuse to be daunted by possible vetos from theologians, what hints might we glean from a more imaginative approach to Christ's resurrection and our own resurrection?

A great deal is at stake here. The possibility of introducing a theme into our prayer seems linked with the possibility of exercising our imagination about it. Even if images appear to contribute relatively little to our prayer at a given moment, nevertheless we can hardly pray about something unless our imagination can get hold of it. To parody Wittgenstein: "Whereof we have no imagination, thereof we have no prayer." Many find it easier to contemplate the life and passion of Jesus rather than his resurrection. Their imagination gets left out in the cold, once they move beyond Good Friday.

Amos Wilder recently observed: "Imagination is a necessary component of all profound knowing and celebration. . . . It is at the level of the imagination that any full engagement with life takes place."[2] His remarks bear on prayer. It could well be that the lack of images to shape and motivate contemplation of the resurrection has stopped many from celebrating that mystery profoundly in their prayer and becoming fully engaged with it.

Artists and Contemplatives

Art and contemplation suggest two avenues of approach. First of all, painters and sculptors can entice us to reflect on the risen life more imaginatively and with less cool rationalism. Great artists create symbols through which we can share an experience. They invite us to renew in our imagination the work of their imagination. In dealing with the human body, artists as different as El Greco and Rodin discover and set free a kind of second body. They go behind the familiar appearance of the human body to re-express it in a new way. They disengage from the organic, material bodies before

them—not mere replicas in which we can discern a
likeness, but hidden things of splendor and beauty.
They discover an inner glory in their subjects and,
as it were, transcribe them into another world. The
creative intuitions and hands of the artists liberate a
new life within ordinary life. Art, in short, subli-
mates the dull-looking reality of human bodies.

St. Paul repeatedly speaks of God the Father as
having raised Jesus from the dead (Gal. 1:1; 1
Thess. 1:9ff.; Rom. 10:9, etc.). He cautions the
Corinthians against fornication by recalling their
bodily destiny: "God raised the Lord and will also
raise us up by his power" (1 Cor. 6:14). Dare we
represent God the Father as the supreme artist who
has discovered and set free Jesus' final bodily glory
and will do the same for us? In sublimating in this
way his crucified Son he promises to transcribe us
into the splendor and beauty of what Paul calls the
"spiritual body" (1 Cor. 15:44). Some minds at least
can move with natural ease from the lesser wonder
of artistic creation to the greater wonder of God's
new creation. The resurrection is seen as nothing
less than the great artist discovering and disengag-
ing our hidden body of glory.

Paul encourages such an imaginative leap from
the lesser to the greater when he recalls an analogy
from his Jewish background. Even dull readers, he
expects, can marvel at the growth from grain to
harvest.

Someone will ask, how are the dead raised?
With what kind of body do they come? You

foolish man! What you sow does not come to life unless it dies. And what you sow is not the body which is to be, but a bare kernel, perhaps of wheat or of some other grain. But God gives it a body he has chosen, and to each kind of seed its own body (1 Cor. 15:35-38).

Here Paul invites his readers—for all their foolishness—to make the leap from the lesser miracle of harvest to the great wonder of the risen life:

So it is with the resurrection of the dead. What is sown is perishable, what is raised is imperishable. It is sown in weakness, it is raised in power. It is sown a physical body, it is raised a spiritual body (1 Cor. 15:42-44).

In his preaching, Jesus never observes, "The spiritual, risen body will be like unto. . . ." Nevertheless, his parables and, in general, his teaching anticipate the route of the Pauline imagination in 1 Corinthians—a movement from the lesser to the greater. Marriage feasts symbolize the big party God will throw at the end of time. Travelers turning up late at night and looking for food suggest the nature of prayer to God. A father's loving welcome to a renegade son serves to picture the divine mercy. Sunshine and rain reflect God's free generosity to all alike—the just and the unjust, the good and the evil. Over and over again Jesus asks his listeners to let the ordinary things and events around them become the means for understanding and accepting God's activity on their behalf.

Of course, our great knowledge of botany and agriculture can get in the way of entering enthusiastically into Paul's particular example. Genetics, fertilizers and tractors have sapped the wonders of the harvest. All the same, we may substitute other examples and imitate Paul and Jesus in jumping from the ordinary or extraordinary things of human experience to the objects of our faith and hope. In particular, the ways that great artists render the human body can make some sense of what risen existence could be like.

Reflection on genuine contemplatives, ascetics and mystics may also yield a hard nugget of imaginative truth about resurrection life. True contemplatives and ascetics, both Christian and non-Christian, give up a number of normal human activities. They substitute hours of prayer for usual occupations. They may sleep less than others. They often engage in fasting. Many renounce marriage. Some stay in one place. All in all, they abandon much that seems to make earthly existence worthwhile. Yet far from living less than others, they appear in some ways to live more. Their asceticism looks like a putting to death. But at least in the case of genuine ascetics and contemplatives this apparent "mortification" is really a "vivification." Remarkable powers of energy and spiritual insight are released. Pain and fear lose their grip. A new freedom arises to overcome the limitations of ordinary lives. The mind and will function in ways that go beyond what men and women normally experience.

I am thinking here not just of extraordinary phenomena like ecstasy, second sight or the power to work miracles. The story of such a non-visionary and down to earth person as Dietrich Bonhoeffer shows how this deeply prayerful and self-disciplined man, while seeming to live "less," in fact lived "more." The "mortification" that was truly a "vivification" comes through the material he wrote as a prisoner in a Nazi jail. A luminous freedom shone round him at the end. The prison doctor who witnessed the execution on a spring morning in 1945 said later:

On the morning of that day between five and six o'clock the prisoners . . . were taken from their cells, and the verdicts of the court-martial read out to them. Through the half-open door in one room of the huts I saw Pastor Bonhoeffer, before taking off his prison garb, kneeling on the floor praying fervently to his God. I was most deeply moved by the way this lovable man prayed, so devout and so certain that God heard his prayer. At the place of execution, he again said a short prayer and then climbed the steps to the gallows, brave and composed. His death ensued after a few seconds. In the almost fifty years that I worked as a doctor, I have hardly ever seen a man die so entirely submissive to the will of God.[3]

Events like these let our thoughts dart forward to

the risen life. The resurrected shape of things to
come casts its light before it.

Like countless contemplatives, ascetics and
mystics, Jesus passed by much that seems to make
human life valuable. He never married, confined his
active career to a year or two spent in a pocket
handkerchief country, and cut sleep short to spend
hours in prayer while the world which he challenged
to repent rapidly turned dangerous. In a great many
ways Jesus came across as someone who lived
"less" than others—that "son of man" who had
"nowhere to lay his head" (Mt. 8:20). Yet he was
remembered as the one from whom power came
forth to heal people (Mk. 5:30). Even if no
evangelist ever described his physical appearance,
nevertheless they recalled one occasion during his
ministry when bright glory shone through Jesus:

> And after six days Jesus took with him Peter
> and James and John, and led them up a high
> mountain apart by themselves; and he was
> transfigured before them, and his garments be-
> came glistening, intensely white, as no fuller on
> earth could bleach them (Mk. 9:2ff.).

In brief, such luminous and powerful moments
in the lives of people like Dietrich Bonhoeffer,
Teresa of Avila or Francis of Assisi—not to mention Jesus himself—can offer memorable glimpses
of what resurrection life might be like. These occasions form living parables when the gap between the

here and the hereafter closes a little and we can say, "The resurrection will be like unto the moment when. . . ."[4]

Physics and Biology

Science delivers some satisfactory possibilities in our quest for images of the resurrection. First, the surprising fact that seemingly inert matter contains such immense energy holds out one approach. Nuclear physics vindicated the truth of Einstein's equation: Energy equals mass by the speed of light squared ($E = MC^2$). Can we put aside any qualms, take advantage of this wonder of nature and once again move from the lesser to the greater in picturing the resurrection? As man has learned to set free stunning amounts of power from tiny pieces of matter, so God took the dead Jesus and liberated him to be the risen Lord, one powerfully present to all times and places. In a sense, unintended by the author, St. Paul's words apply here: "It is sown in weakness, it is raised in power" (1 Cor. 15:43). An apparently weak lump of matter can explode with such energy. Is it too much to use this "miracle" of nuclear physics as an image of Jesus being utterly "weak" in death and then transformed to such power through his resurrection? Reason may tug at our elbow and say that this use of our imagination is absurd. But a hundred years ago, or even less, reason would have declared Einstein's equation absurd.

We may also be able to respond with sympathy and understanding to suggestions coming from modern biology. Once upon a time people naively assumed a far-reaching autonomy and stability for the human body. They had not yet discovered that our life is a dynamic process of constant circulation between our bodies and our environment. Xavier Léon-Dufour puts it this way:

> In the universe there circulates a total body of "materials" which are the object of unceasing exchanges. For example, of the sixty million, million cells which compose the human organism, five hundred million are renewed every day. . . . My body is the universe received and made particular in this instant by myself.[5]

To adapt John Donne's words, no body is an island.

Now the point of comparison with the resurrection is this: In being raised from the dead, Jesus was liberated to enter into a web of relationships "with the universe of men and things."[6] Such language may seem an improbable piece of religious poetry. Yet talk about millions of cells being exchanged every day between the human body and the universe probably still sounds to many like an improbable piece of biological poetry. Can we make the leap from the lesser marvel to the greater one — from the world of interrelated organisms to the risen Christ's intense interrelationship with the entire universe? In his bodiliness he was freed from the ordinary limitations of space, time and matter to enjoy relations with all times and places. What is true of all resurrected persons holds true all the more of Jesus Christ: no risen body is an island.

Here one crashes up against a difficulty I raised in my *The Resurrection of Jesus Christ*.[7] The images drawn from physics and biology highlight the transformation effected through resurrection. Matter becomes energy. A network of organic relationships with the world is uniquely enhanced. The more profound the transformation brought about by resurrection, the more problematic becomes the task of illustrating the continuity between the new risen life and the old earthly existence. If our images prove successful in suggesting Christ's transformation, the identification between the risen Christ and the earthly Jesus becomes doubtful. Yet the risen Lord never says, "I was Jesus," still less, "I come in place of Jesus." But he announces, "It is I myself" (Lk. 24:39). Can modern science provide some help toward coping, not only with the transformation, but also with the continuity involved in resurrection?

A footnote tucked away at the back of Léon-Dufour's book lets a possible answer emerge.[8] What keeps human organisms intact and preserves their continuity, despite the astonishing ebb and flow of cells, is their genetic structure. At that level what supports an enduring identity is something quite small, if extraordinarily complex: a pattern of coded macromolecules. The point of comparison would be this: An invisible factor, the structure of our genetic constitution, preserves our continuity in the face of a rapid flux of materials. Likewise the continuity between our *ante-mortem* and *post-mortem* existence rests on God's action in raising and enhancing such an element of structure. An invisible formula (a lesser marvel) can keep identity intact in the face of the massive changes demanded by our present organic existence. Can we toy with the notion of a greater marvel—God resurrecting—and transmuting some such formula in ways that will make the wonders of modern physics and biology seem like child's play?

Thus far I have been pressing the case for engaging our imagination when we tackle the question: What could the resurrection possibly be like? The style of argument adopted by Jesus and—at times—by St. Paul can encourage this approach. So too does Plato. After pages of close debate about philosophical issues he introduced myths into several of his great dialogues. He did this, I suspect, not to round matters off with a "mere" literary device, but to coax his audience into some primordial insights. Plato's practice implies that poetic visions, no less than philosophical argumentation, can lead us into the truth. We should engage the imagination as a partner in our search for religious understanding and not dismiss it as a threat to clear thinking.

Some readers, however, may hold that with the resurrection, if anywhere, we should be content to accept God's astonishing power and leave it quietly at that. We might want to take our cue from that haunting remark of St. Ignatius of Antioch: "Christ rose in the silence of God." Surely our awed silence

is preferable here to ceaseless chatter. We may feel
like that astronaut who remarked about his col-
league, "Yes, he's all right, if a bit inclined to throw
his weightlessness about." Is the whole range of
comparisons—from nuclear physics to St. Paul's
reflections on the harvest—ultimately weightless?
After all, the resurrection is the mysterious object
of faith and not a theme of scientific knowledge.

Finally readers must decide for themselves
whether the images proposed above do in fact
enlighten and strengthen their resurrection belief.
Only they can tell if the comparisons drawn from
art, contemplation, nuclear physics and biology actually work.

At the same time, from its beginnings Christian
literature has favored efforts to apprehend divine
mysteries through images drawn from the world of
our senses. Ignatius of Antioch may warn us to be
cautiously quiet about the resurrection. Nevertheless, the same bishop in the following terms asks the
Roman Christians not to block his martyrdom: "Let
me be the food of wild beasts, for they shall bring
me to God. I am God's wheat, and the teeth of
beasts will grind me into Christ's pure bread." This
is lively imagery to express what he calls his "approaching birth" into real life when he will be "truly
man" and "see the pure Light." Ignatius endorses
both approaches to the resurrection—imaginative
boldness, no less than reverent restraint.

Some readers, however, may flinch from
examples which draw on "things out there" and
have a strong imaginative impact. They may, in-

stead, be helped by some suggestions coming from modern philosophy which touch experience "in here." Admittedly the images so far introduced, especially those from modern science, have a strong physical flavor. Several hints from the philosophers look more to the human person. These possibilities may soften prejudices against trying to throw light on the resurrection. Let me suggest four such approaches—under the headings of "love," "freedom," "thought," and "sex."

Love, Freedom, Thought, and Sex

First of all, love is the language of "forever." Gabriel Marcel has been invoked here a thousand times, but one more time will not hurt. His reflections on love eloquently support the conclusion, "To love someone is to say, 'You will not die.'" Love does not tolerate limits imposed by time or death. We would find it unaccountably odd of parents to assure their children, "We shall love you all but only for fifteen years." What would we make of children who told their parents, "We shall forget you, once you are dead"? We could only shake our heads in puzzlement over a lover who said to his beloved, "I will love you for five years." Genuine love is committed and committing to the language of "forever."

This love of men and women hints at the divine love exhibited in the resurrection. For God the Father to say "This is the Son whom I love" (see

Mk. 1:11; 9:7) was to say "He will not die" or, rather, "I will not abandon him to death" (Acts 2:25-31). Human beings speak brave words of love, but know their weakness in the face of death. The Father's word of love, however, was powerful when he spoke it over the corpse laid to rest near Calvary: "You will not die forever."

St. John points us in this direction. The second half of his Gospel focuses on the passion, death and resurrection of Jesus. It is precisely then that the language of love comes to the fore. Chapters 13-20 use the word "love" (both noun and verb) four times as often as do Chapters 1-12. As the crucifixion looms up and the resurrection happens, the evangelist reaches naturally for love-language. We can adapt a famous text of the Gospel to express our point: Having always loved his Son who was in the world, the Father now showed the full extent of his love (Jn. 13:1). The truth Marcel enunciated reached its classic fulfillment when the Father's love raised the dead Jesus to a new life of glory.[9] In short, one might echo St. Augustine and cry out here: "Give me a lover and he will understand the resurrection."

Freedom holds out other possible ways of pondering the resurrection. In *The Resurrection of Jesus Christ* I developed one such approach. The risen person finds himself or herself "permanently liberated from all perverse, death-dealing forces, be they death itself, sin, suffering and oppression of various kinds." As well as this "freedom from," I noted a "freedom for" which resurrection brings:

[The risen Christ] has ceased to be an object in our world which can be sought out and confronted at will. As the Damascus-road event dramatically illustrates, Christ has become free to present himself or not. With sovereign freedom he initiates the episode and of his own accord emerges from his hiddenness to show himself where and to whom he wishes (p. 115).

Both these points touched Christ's new freedom. However, we can also think of the Father's freedom. Let me explain.

For years we may wonder whether we live truly free lives. The opportunity—or even better the invitation—to do something new can restore our confidence that we have not lost the courage to exercise our liberty. Some people can feel a pressing personal need to break loose and prove their freedom to themselves. Doing something new and, as far as they are concerned, unique can happily meet that need.

Now it would be bizarre to portray God the Father experiencing some pressing personal need to exercise his freedom and then meeting that need by raising Jesus from the dead. All the same, the resurrection presents us with God doing something utterly new and quite unique. Easter Sunday witnesses to the creative liberty of God. The God who freely called all things into existence now freely calls back, into a new existence, a human being who once existed and is now dead. The wonder of the original creation recedes before the wonder of the new creation. The fresh and final future to which Christ's resurrection testifies lets us see the over-riding freedom of God who promises, "Behold, I make all things new" (Rev. 21:5).

To sum up: We can turn to advantage contemporary convictions about the high value of freedom and the need to keep freedom alive. God asserts a unique divine freedom through an astonishingly new act, the resurrection of the crucified Jesus.

Teilhardian terminology provides another avenue for approaching the resurrection. The mutation from the biosphere to the noosphere is a lesser image of the greater mutation—from the noosphere to what can be called the pneumatosphere, or realm of the spirit. The first mutation brought the appearance of thought. Human thought can embrace the universe. It can reach out instantly across millions of miles of space or back through endless centuries of time. But human activity fails to keep pace with thought. Our actions remain pinned down and engulfed by the universe. The transformation which came with the appearance of thought has not yet occurred for human activity. Can we imagine resurrection as a mutation from the noosphere to the pneumatosphere, such as will bring for human action the kind of metamorphosis which has already taken place for human thought?

Lastly, human sexuality helps to make sense of the resurrection. All too often, of course, the Christian Church and—for that matter—other religious groups have had to face the perversions to which sinful men and women have put their sexuality. It is hardly to be expected that believers will leap head-long to embrace sex as a symbol of the resurrection. For its part, modern science has been busy dismantling taboos about sexuality, as well as trivializing that whole dimension of human existence. The successors of Kinsey would not normally care to classify and research *vestigia resurrectionis* (traces of the resurrection) in their chosen area of specialization.

Even if neither religion nor science is likely to favor his observations, Jean Guitton has rightly singled out two aspects of sexual life which come across as *vestigia resurrectionis*: union and ecstasy. Sexual love means leaving the limits of one's own existence and being united in peaceful ecstasy with another. Resurrection entails a transformation that maximizes both elements. The risen person in an enduring ecstasy breaks free to enjoy union with God and the world. The mystical tradition of Christianity long ago pressed the Canticle of Canticles into service and drew from sexual love images for expressing higher forms of prayer life. I can still remember my astonishment when I flicked through a book by St. Bernard and struck phrases like "between the breasts of the beloved," "the kiss of the mouth," "the bedchamber of the Bridegroom" and other exotic words filling out Bernard's picture of what the spiritual marriage between Christ and the Christian means. He saw such mystic experiences on earth as anticipating heavenly glory. The marriage which starts here would be consummated hereafter. Bernard had scriptural warrant for such imagery—not just the Canticle of Canticles but the vision in Revelation: "I saw the holy city, new Jerusalem, coming down out of heaven from God, prepared as a bride adorned for her husband" (Rev. 21:2). Guitton would invite us to take a cue from Bernard and the Bible and find in the ecstatic union of sexual love some memorable *vestigia resurrectionis*.

This chapter has indicated possibilities which may have enough variety and vitality to get our imaginations to work on the resurrection. Such an exercise of our fantasy may let the resurrection come alive for us. Despite warnings from Hume and the theologians, nothing may let the paschal mystery more successfully engage our life of prayer than controlled flights of the imagination.

4
Further Growth Points

Reading and reflection over the past ten years have brought to my notice a curious phenomenon concerning Christ's resurrection and its aftermath. On the one hand, many non-Roman Catholic theologians and exegetes agree that at the outset of Christianity St. Peter functioned as the primary witness to Easter. This view is expressed—albeit with different nuances—by Hans Conzelmann, C. F. Evans, R. H. Fuller and Willi Marxsen, to name just a few.[1] I do not wish to flood the reader with names and references. A statement from Peter Selby (an Anglican) exemplifies this widespread consensus: "It is clear from the Pauline tradition as well as from other evidence that there was a strong tradition that there was a first appearance of the risen Lord to Peter, and that this determined to some extent the position which Peter came to hold within the life of the Church."[2]

On the other hand, however, no Roman Catholic that I know of has ever taken Peter's role as resurrection witness as the foundation out of which to construct a theology of the Petrine ministry and the papacy. Those sturdy Counter-Reformation defenders of the papacy, Suarez (1548-1617) and St. Robert Bellarmine (1542-1621), did not do so. In the case of Suarez this is all the more surprising, as he wrote fairly extensively on the resurrection. Both before and after the Reformation, Catholic attention has regularly been caught by Matthew's "Thou art Peter" or John's "Feed my lambs, feed my sheep." These are the texts written high on the walls of St. Peter's Basilica in Rome. One looks in vain for Luke's "The Lord has risen indeed and has appeared to Simon."

In this chapter I plan to sketch two issues that cry out for attention: (1) Peter's witness to Christ's resurrection as the right point of departure for a theology of the papacy, and (2) women and the paschal mystery. To conclude, I want to indicate rapidly several other resurrection themes which invite further consideration. This wrapup will involve a fast mixture of uneven materials, but there is no way to avoid this without going beyond the scope of this volume.

Peter as Easter Witness

The list of resurrection witnesses in 1 Corinthians places first Christ's appearance to Peter: "He appeared to Cephas, then to the Twelve" (1 Cor. 15:5). Luke confirms this priority of Peter as Easter witness in a traditional formulation which he introduces somewhat awkwardly at the end of the Emmaus story: "The Lord has risen indeed, and has appeared to Simon'' (Lk. 24:34). Seemingly Luke inserts this item to prevent any impression that the Emmaus appearance was the primary one. Even before Cleopas and his companion returned, Peter's testimony brought to Easter-faith "the Eleven" and "those who were with them" (Lk. 24:33). The later appearances of the Lord strengthened this faith and did not create it for the first time. Luke has prepared his readers for all this by Jesus' promise at the Last Supper that, when Peter had "turned again," he was to "strengthen" his brethren (22:32). The primary appearance to Peter explains his prominence in Acts 1-12. Luke can thus bridge the gap between the ministry of Jesus and the history of the early Church in which Peter served as leader.

Before going further let me hasten to add that by speaking of Peter as primary Easter witness I am thinking only of the appearances to those who were to become "official proclaimers of the resurrection."[3] John's Gospel reports Mary Magdalene as being the one to whom the Lord first appeared, and she brought the good news to the disciples: "I have seen the Lord" (Jn. 20:14-18). According to Matthew, Mary Magdalene and "the other Mary" met Jesus as they returned from discovering the empty tomb (Mt. 28:9f.). This brief encounter is the first appearance of the risen Lord recorded by Matthew. Mary Magdalene and other women followers of Jesus belonged to the core group which set the Church going. One can speak of them as the "founding mothers" alongside the "founding fathers" of the Christian community. Nevertheless, it was Peter who took the primary role as official proclaimer of the Lord's resurrection. In that sense I wish to refer to his priority as Easter witness.

We find a further suggestion of this Petrine priority in Mark's Gospel where the angel instructs the women: 'Go, tell his disciples and Peter that he is going before you to Galilee; there you will see him'' (Mk. 16:7). Here the Easter story reaches its climax neither with the discovery of the empty tomb nor even with the angel's announcement of the resurrection, but with the command to communicate the good news to the ''disciples and Peter.'' Only Peter gets singled out for mention by name. Fuller believes that 'the naming of Peter as well as the disciples . . . indicates clearly that the evangelist is alluding to the two appearances listed in 1 Corinthians 15:5—namely, the appearance to 'Cephas' and to 'the Twelve.' ''[4]

John's Gospel, albeit with qualifications, also reflects Peter's status as primary witness to the Lord's resurrection. When Mary Magdalene discovers the empty tomb, she runs to inform ''Simon Peter and the other disciple, the one whom Jesus loved.'' They both visit and inspect the grave (Jn. 20:1-10). The appendix to the fourth Gospel (Chapter 21) acknowledges Peter's function as resurrection witness and the pastoral role he receives from the risen Lord. Peter has taken six others out for a night's fishing. Dawn brings an encounter with the Lord on the shore. After breakfast Christ commissions Peter to feed his ''lambs'' and ''sheep.'' Here

Peter is established as "shepherd" of his Lord's flock on the far side of the resurrection.

Both Chapters 20 and 21 of John modify somewhat the place of Peter as primary Easter witness. The specifically "Johannine" testimony receives some degree of priority. In the race to the empty tomb the beloved disciple both outruns Peter and comes to believe, as he enters the tomb and sees the grave cloths tidily arranged. It looks as if John's Gospel wants to represent the beloved disciple as first to believe. Chapter 21 likewise qualifies Peter's prominence as resurrection witness. The beloved disciple recognizes the stranger on the beach, even if it is Peter who first wades ashore to meet the risen Christ. The same beloved disciple will outlive Peter to continue the Easter testimony till the end of the apostolic age (Jn. 21:18ff.). Nevertheless, Peter's priority as Easter witness remains substantially unchallenged in Chapter 21. Moreover in Chapter 20 a hint of deference toward this role of his can be spotted when the beloved disciple waits for Peter before entering the empty grave (Jn. 20:3ff.).

Peter in the New Testament assesses carefully these (and further) data about Peter. That important study, sponsored by the United States Lutheran-Roman Catholic Dialogue, speaks of "the important tradition about Peter having been the first of the major companions of Jesus' ministry to have seen the Lord after the resurrection" and concludes that "it is very likely that such a tradition provided the original context or catalyst for much of the New

Testament material about Peter.''[5] Because of its
scope, however, this book does not construct a theology of the Petrine ministry on the basis of that
tradition about Peter's priority as resurrection witness. It ends simply by tracing various "images of
Peter in New Testament thought": Peter as missionary, as pastor, as martyr, as guardian of the
faith and so forth. His priority as Easter witness
gets tucked away with the theme (developed in
Christian apocryphal literature) of Peter as "the re-
ceiver of special revelation.''[6]

So far we have been recalling various New Testament items which converge to suggest Peter's
priority among those who see the Lord after the
resurrection. Luke in his Gospel and in Acts illustrates that we are dealing with more than a merely
chronological priority which lacks theological significance. There the risen Christ's subsequent appearances to groups or individuals confirm what has
already been accepted through Peter. His Easter
faith leads others to believe and gathers into a new
community the bewildered followers of Jesus. In
Acts Peter steps forward repeatedly to proclaim the
good news that God has raised up Jesus of Nazareth
who has been "crucified and killed by the hands of
lawless men'' (Acts 2:22-24). Two stages are involved here! Simon experiences the Lord in his
risen glory and becomes Peter, the fundamental
witness to the joyful news of Easter. Confronted
with the risen Christ, he takes up his essential function of announcing that resurrection.

What conclusions would all this imply for those

who take a biblical basis for interpreting the position of the Bishop of Rome? What morals might we draw to elucidate the nature of the papacy? Ultimately, this way of understanding the Petrine ministry leads to a primary stress on witness rather than on jurisdiction. The Pope succeeds to Peter in his rôle as fundamental witness to Christ's resurrection. *The* key becomes primacy of witness to the paschal mystery rather than primacy of any legal authority. We can thus appreciate the function of the Pope against the background of Peter's testimony to Christ's victory (found in the early chapters of Acts) rather than against the background of Peter's authoritative position at the Council of Jerusalem in Acts 15. Undoubtedly, the fundamental witness to the Lord's resurrection must also responsibly guide, govern and teach. But it would be inverting the sequence of importance to insist first on jurisdiction and public authority.

The Catholic theology of the papacy which led up to and derived from Vatican I has turned its attention to the primacy of papal jurisdiction and the (rarely exercised) personal infallibility of the Pope. Standard textbooks of ecclesiology have taken up the Vatican I definition about Christ "promising" to Peter and then "conferring" on him "the primacy of jurisdiction" (Denzinger-Schönmetzer, n. 3053), but failed to notice the decisive events which took place between that promise and the conferral. Christ died, rose and appeared to Peter who assumed the role of fundamental witness to the resurrection. For standard Catholic ecclesiology it is intrinsically irrelevant that the "conferral" took place after Easter. It would be the same if early in the ministry Christ had promised the primacy to Peter and then conferred it as part of the ceremony at the Last Supper.

Universal negatives are notoriously dangerous, but I know no Catholic theologian or writer who clearly fastens on the priority of witness to Christ's resurrection as *the* key to the Petrine and papal ministry. Andrew Greeley got closer than anyone when he wrote:

> As a symbol, the papacy must stand for conviction and confidence—conviction that the Suffering Servant had indeed become the Son of Man, and that through suffering and death man comes to resurrection. The pope must be the prime "celebrant" of Christianity, a man who presides over the joyous festivities that ought to mark the Christian conviction that life has triumphed over death.[7]

"Symbol" recalls for me a yearly ceremony that quite literally enacts the theology of papacy for which I am asking. Each year millions of people see on television or hear on the radio the Pope's Easter broadcast. In different languages the Pope announces to the city of Rome and to the world the glorious news that lies at the heart of Christianity: "Christ is risen, Alleluia!" There exists an extraordinary gap between this proclamation and that Catholic theology which focuses on the issue of universal, "ordinary" jurisdiction. In a special way each year, the Pope visibly serves and strengthens the Church's faith by re-enacting before all mankind the role of Peter, the fundamental witness to Easter.

To sum up: It would enrich Catholic ecclesiology if those who treated the Petrine ministry and papal office could stop moving instinctively to the primacy of jurisdiction as the fundamental issue. Matthew 16:13-19 and John 21:15-17—or rather the traditional exegeses of those passages—have too long dominated the discussion both among those who maximize and among those who minimize papal jurisdiction. It would at least be worth trying to swing free from those classic texts and test out as the biblical starting point Luke 24:34 and Peter's speeches in Acts (3:15; 4:10; 10:40f., etc.). If this proposal makes some people nervous about the theory and practice of Church authority, it has one huge advantage, in that it links the papal role firmly to the basic message of Christianity: "Jesus is risen!"

Women and the Paschal Mystery

A second growth point which deserves attention from contemporary theology concerns what I call the feminine face of Jesus' death and resurrection. We can develop this theme from the text of the Gospels according to John and Mark.

First, let us consider the presentation in John. During his farewell discourse Jesus assured his dis-

ciples that their sorrow would be replaced by a
unique joy. To express his promise he cited the experience of childbirth:

> You will weep and lament, but the world will
> rejoice; you will be sorrowful, but your sorrow
> will turn into joy. When a woman is in travail
> she has sorrow, because her hour has come;
> but when she is delivered of the child, she no
> longer remembers the anguish, for joy that a
> child is born into the world. So you have sor-
> row now, but I will see you again and your
> hearts will rejoice, and no one will take your
> joy from you (Jn. 16:20-22).

At the crucifixion itself, so John informs his
readers, the mother of Jesus was standing with the
other women. She said nothing, but stood there silently to see the end. Jesus gave her into the care of
the beloved disciple with the words, ''Woman, behold your son'' (Jn. 19:25-27). On Easter Sunday
Mary Magdalene found the tomb empty, passed on
news of her startling discovery, and returned to
weep at the hollowed out place where the corpse of
Jesus had been laid. Then near the place of death
and burial Jesus appeared to her and asked:
''Woman, why are you weeping?'' (Jn. 20:15).
When he identified himself by calling Mary Magdalene by name, ecstatic joy replaced this woman's
pain.

A feminine sequence emerges clearly from
John's text. From the image of a woman in

childbirth, we move to the mother standing with other women by the cross to see her Son die. And we come finally to the woman whose sorrow was turned into joy. Near the tomb, that "vessel" which received Jesus' torn body and like a womb held it for three days, she encountered Christ newly and gloriously alive.

At times commentators on the Gospels have contented themselves with merely "factual" questions. How strong is the evidence that Jesus' mother attended the crucifixion? Did Mary Magdalene and/or other women discover the tomb to be empty on the third day? Such questions of fact risk ignoring deeper levels of symbolic meaning in the Gospel texts which relate the events of Good Friday and Easter Sunday. It may prove hard to catch this meaning in a net of words, but we cannot bypass the task of reflecting on the feminine face of Jesus' death, burial and resurrection.

However, before drawing three such reflections from John's text, I need to insert several disclaimers. First, the fourth evangelist was probably far from fully appreciating the import and weight of the symbolic language that characterizes his Gospel. But the explicit intention of an author is not essential for our interpretation. Here I agree with those like H. G. Gadamer who do not allow the primary question to be "Was this meaning in the mind of the author?" Rather they ask, "Is this meaning in the text?" Second, symbols can suggest, express and typify a whole range of meaning. But no rational "explanation" can ever hope to capture

this range of meaning, let alone state some clearly
defined meaning(s) which everyone feels to be present. Hence just as I am not claiming to pinpoint some
theme consciously worked out by an evangelist, so I
would not pretend to exhaust the symbolic meaning
to be found in the Gospel texts. Third, I realize that
"feminine" and "masculine" are principles of
being human. Even if a woman in her capacity to
bear children and in other ways expresses for us the
"feminine," we should identify neither feminine
with female nor masculine with male.

   After these disclaimers let me make three ten-
tative reflections on the feminine imagery in John's
passion and resurrection story. First of all, women
and feminine imagery surround the dying and rising
of Jesus. From the appeal to the experience of
childbirth in his final discourse we move to the
mother and other women silently present at the
place and event of death. Then near the tomb-womb
one of the women becomes the first person to meet
Christ in his new and final state of risen existence.
Women enclose the paschal mystery. This suggests
something about our prayerful access to Good Friday and Easter Sunday. To know this mystery we
need to know it in a feminine way. We could parody
Augustine and say: Show me a woman and she will
understand Christ's death and resurrection. We return to this first point when we take up Mark's narrative.

   My second reflection on what I call the
feminine face of the crucifixion and resurrection in
John focuses on Jesus himself. Long before this

Gospel was written, Old Testament books used the figure of birth pangs when they announced that God would finally intervene to save his people: for instance, in Isaiah 26:17f. and 66:7-14. In the event this saving intervention takes the form of a crucifixion in which *Jesus* himself suffers birthpangs as he brings the whole human race to new life. His own image of a woman in labor whose sorrow will give way to joy when her baby is "born into the world" is especially exemplified in Jesus himself. He is the woman whose hour has come and who must endure the anguish of birth. Through suffering the pain of Calvary he gives new life to the world. His mother, Mary Magdalene and other women assist at this agonizing childbirth. In a letter to his troublesome Galatians Paul reaches for the figure of a mother in childbirth to describe his own apostolic experience: "My little children, with whom I am again in travail until Christ be formed in you. . . ." (4:19). The use of such an image in John 16:20-22 encourages us to view Christ's decisive act of salvation within the same feminine perspective.

Third, if we think of Jesus' own mother as the "woman in travail," the immediate result of Calvary is a dead Son. Some artistic representations of the taking down from the cross portray the body of Jesus as very much reduced in size. He lies in his mother's arms almost like a stillborn child. These artists may have spotted something in John's text that commentators missed. The crucifixion "delivers" a dead child, who must be inserted into the tomb before he is finally born to the new life of his risen existence. It is only by passing through the grave that Mary's Son becomes the "first-born from the dead" (Col. 1:18).

Before leaving the feminine face of Jesus' death and resurrection, I want to note a valuable pattern in Mark's Gospel. The essential point is this: Male disciples fail to grasp and enter into the paschal mystery, but female disciples share more and more in the story until they emerge as the first to learn the good news of Easter.

In Chapters 8, 9 and 10 of Mark, Jesus three times speaks about his coming suffering, death and resurrection. On each occasion the male disciples can neither comprehend nor accept the message. Peter tries to rebuke Jesus for predicting such a destiny (Mk. 8:32). As a group the disciples argue about the nature of greatness (Mk. 9:33ff.). James and John request for themselves a place of preeminence in the coming kingdom (Mk. 10:35ff.). Judas agrees to betray Jesus. Peter vehemently denies that he will disown his master. Then when Jesus is arrested in the garden, all these disciples run away. Peter slips into the courtyard of the high priest's house. There he three times denies his master. In Mark's account no male disciple attends the crucifixion. To sum up: The male disciples *talk* a good deal but simply cannot understand or accept Jesus' suffering destiny. Their masculine logic fails to cope with God's mysterious way of saving the world.

Just as the collapse of the male disciples reaches its climax, women take a more prominent role in Mark's story. At a meal in Bethany an anonymous woman comes in and pours costly ointment over the head of Jesus. He defends her against criticism: "She has done what she could; she has anointed my body beforehand for burying" (Mk. 14:3-9). Then Mary Magdalene and "many other women" witness the crucifixion and death of Jesus (Mk. 15:40f.). They also watch when the body is taken down from the cross and buried. At sunrise on the third day Mary Magdalene and two other women visit the tomb. To their amazement they find the stone rolled away from the entrance. They enter the tomb to learn from the interpreting angel the unexpected news: "He has risen, he is not here; see the place where they laid him" (Mk. 16:6). The women then run from the tomb profoundly shaken by the message.

What all this amounts to is: If you think and act feminine, you will seize the mystery of Christ's death and resurrection. Feminine presence and intuition function where masculine talk and logic have failed. A particularly striking element in the whole sequence from Mark 14:3-9 through 16:1-8 is the women's *silence*. Apart from the worry expressed by Mary Magdalene and her companions on the way to the tomb ("Who will roll away the stone for us from the door of the tomb?") nothing is said by any of these women in the final chapters of Mark. They are simply there to share silently in the events. In short, Mark's text suggests a feminine approach to the death and resurrection of Jesus. By wordlessly being there and contemplating the events, we will seize the mystery, or—rather—let the mystery seize us.

Outlandish or acceptable as these musings on John and Mark may be, both Gospel texts confront us with a strong feminine dimension to Christ's dying and rising. Any adequate theological reflection on Good Friday and Easter Sunday should take note of this.[8]

Other Growth Points

To round off this chapter, let me briskly draw attention to a number of themes connected with Christ's resurrection which deserve further study and reflection.

(a) First, let us consider the many-layered unity between his death and resurrection. Karl Barth and Karl Rahner stand out among those theologians who have championed the unity between Good Friday and Easter Sunday. The Lord's dying and rising are distinguishable but never separable. Here what clamors for further study is Holy Saturday. More work is needed both on the so-called "descent into hell" and the nature of death. Despite the contributions from Hans Urs von Balthasar, Ladislaus Boros, William Dalton, Jean Galot and others (including Rahner himself), no firm lines have emerged for a theology of Holy Saturday. The decisive issue seems to be: Should we interpret Christ's "descent into hell" as primarily an *active* or a *passive* episode? For me it rings true to respect fully the passive dimension. Jesus passes into the solitude and inactivity of death. The Word becomes silent for three days—"like the middle stage in a rite of passage . . . which expresses the decisiveness of the change from the former state to the new state."[9]

(b) Scheffczyk's *Auferstehung: Prinzip christlichen Glaubens* overshadows other attempts to show how Christ's resurrection illuminates the whole of Christian faith—or at least major areas of that faith. The resurrection is not just one (important) truth among others. It is the organizing principle for the whole of faith and theology. Scheffczyk exemplifies his thesis by dealing in turn with such doctrines as revelation, the Trinity, the Church, the sacraments, creation and the *eschaton*. His book presents itself as a one-volume *summa* of Christian faith from the standpoint of the Lord's resurrection. This approach deserves further development.

(c) Two other writers have drawn attention to resurrection themes which deeply concern Christian life—what I call Easter morality and Easter prayer. Though so far not widely known in the English-speaking world, Klaus Demmer can only be more and more appreciated for an approach to morality that gives proper weight to the paschal mystery. If Christ's dying and rising are axiomatic for Christian faith, it seems strange to use other grounds for seeking moral truth and deciding on moral action. Should we be satisfied with a calculus of (merely?) human values and not make a calculus of Easter values? Demmer's appeal to the Lord's dying and rising vigorously reminds us that neither for faith nor for morality should we ignore that our being is a being toward death and resurrection. Of course, there are difficulties here. Does the resurrection provide a general vision on life and the motivation for wholehearted engagement, without telling us anything about the rightness or wrongness of specific actions? Whatever our final answer here, any attempt to fashion an Easter morality looks worth the trouble, no matter where the yield comes.

Nearly ten years ago David Stanley published a remarkable study, "Contemplation of the Gospels, Ignatius Loyola, and the Contemporary Christian."[10] This article is woven around four theses. First, there is the conviction of the risen Lord's presence:

> Jesus Christ through his exaltation to the Father's right hand has not been removed to some mythical existence beyond the furthest galaxy, but is *actually more dynamically present in the world* than ever he was when he walked the hills of Galilee.[11]

Second, Stanley insists that this presence entails the present reality of what Jesus experienced in his human history on earth. He writes: "All the mysteries of Jesus' earthly history, from the cradle to the grave, have been mysteriously endowed in his glorified humanity with a totally new and enduring reality."[12] Third, this means that contemplating Jesus' earthly history is a way of relating to him here and now, and not a merely nostalgic reconstruction of something over and done with. Fourth, it is precisely such prayerful assimilation of Jesus' human history that leads us *both* to repeat in our own lives the redeeming experiences of Jesus' own existence *and* to participate personally in the paschal mystery.

The first thesis should win easy acceptance — at least in theory. In practice a sense of the risen Lord's dynamic presence in prayer and spiritual living can be allowed to fade. The third and fourth theses follow reasonably from the second. It is the second which invites deeper study and reflection. Can we explore further the modes in which the experiences of Jesus' earthly history have been actualized forever by his resurrection? What is the "new and enduring *actuality*" that these mysteries have been endowed with? We can only be grateful for what Stanley and others[14] have already offered by way of answer. Every hint deserves to be followed up.

To conclude: This book has moved backward and forward between reporting what "they" have had to say about Christ's resurrection and what I want to say. But what of it? So long as "in every way" the risen Christ is proclaimed, I am content to say with St. Paul: "In that I rejoice" (Phil. 1:18).

Appendix: Willi Marxsen's *The Resurrection of Jesus of Nazareth*

This book is based on a series of open lectures delivered at Münster University in the winter semester of 1967-68. Professor Marxsen's pamphlet *Die Auferstehung Jesu als historisches und als theologisches Problem* (Gütersloh, 1964; translation in *The Significance of the Message of the Resurrection for Faith in Jesus Christ*, edited by C. F. D. Moule, Naperville, 1968) had provoked strong opposition among his fellow Protestants. Hence he decided to present his views at greater length and in a simplified (as well as slightly modified) fashion.

Marxsen begins from the fact that no one in the early Christian community ever claimed to have seen or experienced the resurrection of Jesus as such. There were no eye-witnesses of the resurrection itself. Hence "Jesus is risen" cannot be taken as the direct report of an immediate experience. Such talk of the resurrection was an interpretative statement based on an experience which the first Christians described as "seeing" Jesus and finding faith. It was "only one possible way of expressing the reality of having found faith" (p. 144) and even

106

in early Christianity was replaced by other notions (e.g., exaltation). The concept of the resurrection expressed in pictorial terms "the miraculous nature" of the faith found even after Jesus' death (pp. 141, 156). It seems that after the crucifixion the disciples returned to Galilee and Peter (perhaps while fishing) realized that he was sent forth by Jesus. This "having-found-faith after Good Friday" was externalized into stories of meetings with Jesus after his death. The message of the resurrection, interpreted in visual terms, gave rise to the empty tomb story (pp. 159, 161).

Marxsen himself prefers to describe the miraculous fact that Jesus' "cause" (i.e., his offer of faith) goes on beyond Good Friday by saying, "still he comes today" (p. 147). For "faith after Easter" was and is "no different in substance from that faith to which Jesus had already called men before Easter" (p. 125). Thus the Jesus of the ministry assumes paramount importance. Marxsen eliminates the basis for Christology—the post-Easter proclamation that Jesus had died for our sins and been raised for our salvation. In the events of Good Friday and Easter Sunday the early Christians recognized the turning point of man's history with God and the key motive for acclaiming Jesus as the Christ. Marxsen, however, does not allow for any real difference between the period of Jesus' own preaching and the period when the apostolic preaching of Peter, Paul and the others began. It appears to make little difference for Marxsen's explanation if at the end of his ministry Jesus had suddenly disappeared and never been heard of again. Provided that his words along with some indication of his conduct had been preserved and were now proclaimed to us, we could experience his call and take the risk of faith.

What does Marxsen hold about the present state of Jesus? At times he appears to ascribe to Jesus an active presence in the call to faith which we hear today: "The activity of Jesus . . . goes on in spite of his death on the cross; and it remains the activity of the same Jesus who was once active on earth." For "unlike other peoole belonging to the past, Jesus is not dead but alive" (pp. 77f.), "present in the word of proclamation" (p. 142). In other passages Marxsen seems to terminate Jesus' personal existence on Calvary: *"Jesus is dead. But his offer has not thereby lost its validity"* (italics mine). In this sense Marxsen adopts the formulation "still he comes today" and explains how "he is present today in his offer." "The cause of Jesus" (i.e., "his concern") continues. This past offer of faith is acknowledged, accepted and experienced (pp. 148f.). Marxsen shows himself serenely confident that agnosticism about the facts of Jesus' personal fate will not undermine the validity of his message. "The events following Good Friday (whatever form they took) can detract nothing" from Jesus' challenge (p. 152). The function of our call to faith goes on, no matter what its ontological basis is.

In arguing his case Marxsen is gratifyingly free from existential jargon. The cherished distinction between *Historie* and *Geschichte* nowhere surfaces to irritate some non-German readers. He does not raise the problem of demythologizing the Easter message to render it intelligible to contemporary man. He shows an attractive concern to do justice to the ministry of Jesus and his call to faith. Marxsen rightly values the theme of discipleship, the "follow me" of John 21:19. Essentially the book develops the model of resurrection as faith, but understood—so we shall see—in a particular way.

Marxsen rightly denies that contemporary faith as such forms "an instrument of knowledge which can convey information" about the past event of the resurrection (p. 21). He is ready, however, to argue that faith points to other-worldly realities which impinge on us now: "The man who ventures upon the path [of faith] is bound to acknowledge that Jesus lives. For he has experienced the reality of being called to faith by him. And no believer will deny that this faith is a reality" (p. 142). Does Marxsen simply mean that the man who decides to believe (in the face of the call to faith issued by the historical Jesus) must assert the reality of faith? This would be little more than a tautology: If I decide to believe, I will experience the reality of believing. But if Marxsen wishes to claim that my (real) faith compels me to admit that Jesus himself now lives personally, this argument is obviously open to serious objection. How do I know that I am reading off my experience correctly? Am I perhaps creating for myself an other-worldly person to whom I refer the experience of faith?

Throughout his book Marxsen advises us to

examine the issues carefully, clearly and in a thoroughly unprejudiced way. Yet over and over again passages of cautious (if sometimes skeptical) discussion leap to sudden and unjustified conclusions. Let me give three examples. He points out that the evangelists (apart from Luke) fail to show interest in "the whereabouts of the risen Jesus." John portrays the risen Lord as capable of being touched and yet able to pass through closed doors—attributes that are not "easily reconcilable." The "lack of unity" in the evangelists' "pictures" allows Marxsen to conclude that "the resurrected body of Jesus was simply of no interest at all at the time" (pp. 67f.). There is a breathtaking speed about this deduction which neglects the fact that Luke and John were obviously highly interested in the risen body. In the face of possible or actual Docetic (or Gnostic) denials they went out of their way to insist on the corporeal reality of Jesus' resurrection. In Marxsen's view, since the evangelists fail to depict the resurrected body in exactly the same way, no conclusions may be drawn about the resurrection itself. On the other hand, similar variations become mere "differences of individual viewpoint" which leave "common ground clear enough" when we touch a theme substantial to Marxsen's own thesis—the fact that Jesus' activity (personal? or merely his cause?) continues despite his death. This "identity motif" found in the different Easter stories may be safely preserved, "even though its presentation is individual" (p. 77).

A second example concerns the priority of Peter's faith. Marxsen maintains that we may reasonably conclude that Peter was the first to believe, although it remains "completely unimportant how Peter arrived at his faith in Jesus after Good Friday" (p. 126) since "various versions" of the apostle's coming to faith were passed down. These "various versions" turn out to be essentially only two: 1 Corinthians 15:5, Luke 24:34 and John 21 (all of which report an appearance to Peter), and John 20:3-10 (which describes how Peter and "the other disciple" ran to the empty tomb), a passage which "was probably the work of the evangelist himself." Marxsen asserts that "we are certainly intended to suppose that Peter (who, according to the account, was first inside the tomb) also believed" (pp. 58f.). It is, however, quite doubtful that the text contains any such supposition, let alone "certainly" does so. The demands of a thesis are forcing the exegesis at this point.

My third example bears on Marxsen's shifting attitude toward alternatives. "The point" of the Gospel accounts was "*not* to report the fact that Jesus appeared *but* to explain the reason for making disciples of all nations" (p. 83; italics mine). Here one is not allowed to suggest that these accounts may have intended *both* to report the appearance *and* to explain the mission to all nations. But when dealing with a section of the Pauline formula in 1 Corinthians 15 ("he appeared to the Twelve"), Marxsen disallows any narrowing of the issues through the alternatives: Do we meet here *either* a report of what the Twelve experienced *or* an explanation of the function which the Twelve now have? Such a question is outlawed. At this stage Marxsen can afford to be briefly more tolerant, since he will swiftly argue that "there can be no doubt that Paul understood the formula (even though it does not explicitly mention a function) as function-determining" (pp. 84f.). A few pages later Marxsen declares: "The formula [1 Cor. 15:3ff.] is not aiming to report the number of the appearances. Its intention is to *trace back* the *later* functions and the *later* faith of the Church, as well as the *later* leadership of James to the one single root: the appearance of Jesus" (p. 95; italics mine). Talk of "later leadership" and the "tracing back" of "later functions" and "later faith" suggests quite a gap between the creation of the formula and the events to which it refers. Marxsen remains silent about the date for the formula's composition which many scholars assign to the thirties, and none, I think, after the late forties.

It would be tedious to run through all the points over which I would take issue with Marxsen. Let me list briefly some substantial matters and then turn to the dogmatic position which apparently determines his thesis.

(1) On the basis of Galatians 1:11f. and 16, Marxsen "suspects" that Paul "earlier described" his experience on the Damascus road "in provisional and general terms as revelation" and later—for apologetic reasons—defined this as "seeing" in conformity to "the formulations of the tradition" (pp. 105f.). Marxsen remains silent about Paul's

opening greeting in Galatians (which states that he is an apostle through "Jesus Christ and God the Father who raised him from the dead" (Gal. 1:1). This reference to the resurrection obviously could bear on the claims which Paul goes on to make about the origin, authority and content of the Gospel which he preaches.

(2) Marxsen's exegesis of 1 Corinthians 15:4 proves quite unconvincing. Certainly in 1 Corinthians 15:12-20 Paul is not "offering anything in the nature of factual evidence for the resurrection," nor does he ask the Corinthians to "deduce the factual nature of the resurrection from the existence of faith." But Marxsen's account of this whole section fails to shake the assertion that in verse 14 Paul indicates that "absolutely everything hangs on the resurrection of Jesus as an actual event" (pp. 107-109).

(3) To meet objections to his anti-resurrection thesis, Marxsen must deal with Paul's account of the "earthly body" and the "spiritual body" in 1 Corinthians 15:35-55. Two features of this discussion ought to be challenged. If Marxsen rightly encourages us to translate "body" as "I," he may not gloss over the fact that the "I" in question is a human and hence a bodily existence. Second, he maintains firmly that the risen "I" exists in a form which remains "completely separated" and "totally different" from the mode of existence of the earthly "I." The more seriously one takes this assertion of complete separation and total difference, the more incredible becomes Paul's statement of

"identity of the personality before and after death. Those who rise are the same as those who were alive. It is the same 'I' as it were" (pp. 69f.).

(4) On the empty tomb Marxsen observes: "The opponents of Jesus were unable to 'prove' that the body had been stolen as was the Church to 'prove' that Jesus had risen from the tomb" (p. 167). But, of course, both parties could prove (or at least admit) that the tomb was empty.

(5) Marxsen appears to hold that "the hope of the resurrection of the dead" somehow loses authority through being, "at least in origin, not specifically Christian" and having its "roots" in "ancient Persian ideas which came to be admitted into Judaism" (p. 175). Do those Christian doctrines become second-rate which originated in the Old Testament? Should beliefs of Judaism in their turn be undervalued and even discarded wherever they do not clearly appear to derive from some dramatic communication from Yahweh but may have developed through contact with the religious ideas of non-Israelites? Does Paul's conviction that the resurrection would take place dwindle in importance because this conviction was "part of his outlook as a former Pharisee" (p. 179)?

(6) Finally, Marxsen's understanding of *history* betrays an old-fashioned positivism for which the admissible historical record consists of a concatenation of facts attested by (sense) experience. History deals with "events." These, for Marxsen, must lie within the inherent human possibilities of sense perception and—in principle—be phenomema open to the public.

Marxsen's exegesis inspires less and less confidence as it gradually becomes more obvious that dogmatic convictions are in control. He shows himself definitely cut from a particular kind of traditional Lutheran cloth, and his work forms an attempt to justify on biblical grounds his view of faith. Faith is simply a venture, a commitment made in answer to a call. The alleged legitimation of Jesus' claims through the event of his resurrection would be incompatible with this venture. It is not just that faith goes beyond the evidence; it excludes evidence. Rational appeal would distort faith. To believe because we accepted the testimony of those witnesses who met Jesus alive after his death would render impossible a trusting commitment to Jesus' challenge (pp. 150ff.). From the outset Marxsen resolutely holds apart matters of information and the call to faith (pp. 22f., 30, 110). The historian deals with matters of information and alone decides whether some alleged past event really happened (p. 118). "The historian's answer to the question whether Jesus rose from the dead must be: 'I do not know; I am no longer able to discover' " (p. 119). Even if he were able to answer this question positively, such "isolated talk about the reality of Jesus' resurrection" would constitute a statement apart from faith, simply "the report of a somewhat unusual event" (p. 140). We meet here a sharp distinction between the historian and the believer, an unwarranted separation of the cognitive side of faith from the decision to commit oneself—in a word, a radical isolation of faith from reason.

Bibliography

R. E. Brown, *The Virginal Conception and Bodily Resurrection of Jesus* (New York, 1973).

R. H. Fuller, *The Formation of the Resurrection Narratives* (New York, 1971).

W. Kasper, *Jesus the Christ* (ET: New York, 1976), pp. 124-60.

H. Küng, *On Being a Christian* (ET: New York, 1976), pp. 343-81.

X. Léon-Dufour, *Resurrection and the Message of Easter* (ET: New York, 1975).

W. Marxsen, *The Resurrection of Jesus of Nazareth* (ET: Philadelphia, 1970).

J. Moltmann, *Theology of Hope* (ET: New York, 1967), pp. 133-229.

G. O'Collins, *The Resurrection of Jesus Christ* (Valley Forge, 1973).

N. Perrin, *The Resurrection According to Matthew, Mark, and Luke* (Philadelphia, 1977).

P. Selby, *Look for the Living* (Philadelphia, 1976).

R. C. Ware, "The Resurrection of Jesus," *Heythrop Journal* 16 (1975), pp. 22-35, 174-94.

H. Williams, *True Resurrection* (New York, 1974).

Notes

Chapter 1

1. R. C. Ware. "The Resurrection of Jesus, I: Theological Orientations," *Heythrop Journal* 16 (1975), p. 27. Ware is one of the few writers in English to endorse Klappert's approach or even appear aware of his contribution to the study of the resurrection.

2. Reginald Fuller, *Interpretation* 29 (1975), p. 325.

3. C. F. Evans, *Resurrection and the New Testament* (New York, 1970), p. 130.

4. R. C. Ware, *op. cit.*, p. 183.

5. See further my "Thomas Aquinas and Christ's Resurrection," *Theological Studies* 31 (1970), pp. 512-22.

6. I am aware that some respectable commentators have divided 2 Corinthians into as many as four different letters or fragments of letters. But Werner Kümmel's arguments for the letter's unity (in his *Introduction to the New Testament*) seem to me to be convincing.

7. Karl Barth, *Church Dogmatics IV* 1, pp. 297 ff., 304f. See further my "Karl Barth on Christ's Resurrection," *Scottish Journal of Theology* 26 (1973), pp. 85-99, esp. pp. 94-98. *Church Dogmatics* (1932-68), the masterpiece from the final stage of Barth's theological career, runs to over nine thousand pages in the German original and is thus twice as long as the *Summa* of Thomas Aquinas. Nearly one-third of his enormous work Barth devotes to the redemption or—as he prefers to call it—the atonement.

8. Karl Rahner, "The Eternal Significance of the Humanity of Christ for Our Relationship with God," *Theological Investigations*, Vol. 3 (ET: Baltimore, 1967), pp. 35-46. John O'Brien pointed out to me that, although this early essay (German original 1953) is short and by no means technical, the number of times Rahner refers to it

117

later is quite remarkable. On the full and lasting revelation of God in the glorified Christ, see also J. Alfaro, *Christologia y Antropologia* (Madrid, 1973), pp. 170-82.

9. Wolfhart Pannenberg, *Revelation as History* (ET: New York, 1968), p. 156.

10. For the references, see my *Foundations of Theology* (Chicago, 1971), pp. 31ff.

11. Karl Barth, *The Resurrection of the Dead* (ET: London, 1933), pp. 145-46.

12. Karl Barth, *Epistle to the Romans* (ET: London, 1933), p. 30.

13. Karl Barth, *Church Dogmatics* I/2, *op. cit.*, p. 117.

14. *Ibid.*, III/2, p. 443.

15. Rudolf Bultmann, *Kerygma and Myth*, ed. H. W. Bartsch (New York, 1961), pp. 38ff.

16. Gerhard Ebeling, *The Nature of Faith* (ET: London, 1966), pp. 68ff.

17. Gerhard Ebeling, *Word and Faith* (ET: London, 1963), p. 302; *Theology and Proclamation* (ET: Philadelphia, 1966), p. 91.

18. Peter Selby, *Look for the Living* (Philadelphia, 1976), pp. 171, 135.

19. Jurgen Moltmann, *Theology of Hope* (ET: New York, 1967), p. 190.

20. See my "The Principle and Theology of Hope," *Scottish Journal of Theology* 21 (1968), pp. 129-44.

21. Peter Selby, *op. cit.*, pp. 149, 153f.

Chapter 2

1. Renford Bambrough, *Reason, Truth and God* (London, 1969), p. 79.

2. Peter Selby, *op. cit.*, pp. 89f.

3. Raymond Brown, in *Catholic Biblical Quarterly* 39 (1977), p. 285. The book under review is W. H. Kelber (ed.), *The Passion in Mark: Studies on Mark 14-16* (Philadelphia, 1976).

4. P. F. Strawson, *Meaning and Truth* (Oxford, 1970), p. 5.

5. Here I do not wish to consider the later (canonical) appendix to Mark (16:9-20), which seems to have been added at the beginning of the second century.

6. C. F. Evans, *op. cit.*, p. 84.

7. Raymond Brown, *The Virginal Conception and the Bodily Resurrection of Jesus* (Paulist Press, 1973), pp. 107f. See also his "Difficulties in Using the New Testament in American Catholic Discussion," *Catholic Mind*, Vol. 75, No. 1314 (June 1977), pp. 16f.

8. Xavier Léon-Dufour, *Resurrection and the Message of Easter* (Holt, Rinehart and Winston, 1975), p. 163.

9. John Macquarrie, *The Scope of Demythologizing* (London, 1960), p. 86.

10. Louis Evely, *The Gospels Without Myth* (ET: New York, 1971), p. 165.

11. Peter Selby, *Look for the Living*, p. 98.

12. *Ibid.*

Chapter 3

1. David Hume, *Human Nature*, Bk I, Part IV, Sec. vii.

2. Amos Wilder, *Theopoetic* (Philadelphia, 1976), p. 2.

3. Edward Bethge, *Dietrich Bonhoeffer* (ET: New York, 1970), pp. 830-31.

4. In a somewhat different way J. Guitton develops the images drawn from the work of artists and the lives of the saints as well as a theme we will take up—sexual love as a symbol for resurrection. See his "Epistémologie de la résurrection. Concepts préalables et programme de recherches," in *Resurrexit*, ed. E. Dhanis (Rome, 1974), pp. 108-30.

5. Xavier Léon-Dufour, *op. cit.*, p. 239.

6. *Ibid.*, p. 240.

7. Gerald O'Collins, S.J., *The Resurrection of Jesus Christ, op. cit.*, p. 114.

8. Xavier Léon-Dufour, *op. cit.*, p. 321 n. 42.

9. For the purposes of the argument I have taken the resurrection within the love-dialogue between Father and

Son. I recognize that St. John in places (2:19; 10:17ff.) names Jesus as the agent of his own resurrection.

Chapter 4

1. In his *A Marxist Looks at Jesus* (ET: Philadelphia, 1976) Milan Machovec pays remarkable tribute to the fundamental role played by "Peter's preaching of faith in the exalted Jesus" (pp. 160-65).

2. Peter Selby, *op. cit.*, p. 113.

3. *Peter in the New Testament*, ed. R. E. Brown *et al.* (Minneapolis & New York, 1973), p. 161, n. 340.

4. Reginald Fuller, *The Formation of the Resurrection Narratives* (New York, 1971), pp. 63f.

5. R. E. Brown *et al.*, *Peter in the New Testament, op. cit.*, p. 165.

6. *Ibid.*, pp. 162ff.

7. Andrew Greeley, "Advantages and Drawbacks of a Center of Communications in the Church," *Concilium*, Vol. 4, No. 7 (April 1971), p. 110.

8. For help in reflecting on the feminine face of Jesus' death and resurrection, I wish to thank Sister Kay Leuschner, C.S.J., and other members of my first class at the University of San Francisco.

9. Kieran O'Mahoney in an unpublished thesis on Hans Urs von Balthasar's interpretation of the "descent into hell." I also wish to thank Michael Howlett for making available the results of his research into some contemporary views on the "descent into hell."

10. Cf. *Theological Studies* 29 (1968), pp. 417-43.

11. *Ibid.*, p. 425.

12. *Ibid.*, p. 430.

13. *Ibid.*, p. 428.

14. See K. Rahner, "Mysterien des Lebens Jesu," *Lexikon Für Theologie und Kirche*, Vol. VII (1962), pp. 721f.